UNTOLD MICROCOSMS

First published by Charco Press 2022
Charco Press Ltd., Office 59, 44-46 Morningside Road,
Edinburgh EH10 4BF

ISBN: 9781913867270
e-book: 9781913867287

www.charcopress.com

Coordinated by Carolina Orloff
Edited by Fionn Petch
Cover designed by Pablo Font
Typeset by Laura Jones
Proofread by Fiona Mackintosh

UNTOLD MICROCOSMS

Latin American Writers in the British Museum

Yásnaya Elena A. Gil
Gabriela Cabezón Cámara
Juan Cárdenas
Carlos Fonseca
Lina Meruane
Dolores Reyes
Djamila Ribeiro
Cristina Rivera Garza
Velia Vidal
Joseph Zárate

Translated by
Daniel Hahn • Ellen Jones • Christina MacSweeney
Annie McDermott • Megan McDowell • Robin Myers
Carolina Orloff • Fionn Petch • Frances Riddle • Frank Wynne

Contents

INTRODUCTION

On the Importance of Retelling Stories

The texts that make up this book are all illuminating in their own way. The authors bring their unique perspectives to objects and collections that originally came from Latin America. They take these objects that are loaded with symbolic, political and historical content, and connect them with the present, with their own artistic work and with the here and now of their own countries. *Untold Microcosms* offers a new and challenging look at museum collections, using fictions and personal positions to make visible connections between different collections and diverse local communities, opening up discussions on colonialism, gender studies and Indigenous cultures.

The British Museum's Santo Domingo Centre of Excellence for Latin American Research (SDCELAR) and the Hay Festival invited the authors to take part in this experiment which saw each of them select a piece – or group of pieces – to inspire an original work of narrative. The project seeks to reevaluate how we write about objects in culture and history museums, something that usually takes place with apparent impartiality and strong reliance on academic research and on 'facts'. It also presents a new perspective on the legacy of collecting, questioning the reality that museums continue to manage collections and dominant cultural narratives. That is why in this project we hand over authority to Latin American writers so that they, from their respective positions, interests and imagination, can disturb this purported 'neutrality' and enrich current debates. Part of the creative dialogue between the SDCELAR and the writers is described in the curatorial texts that introduce each of the pieces in this compilation.

The mission of the Hay Festival – which is Welsh in origin, but has a presence in Peru, Mexico, Colombia and the United States – is to reflect on a diverse region that has major differences but shared languages and historical connections. *Untold Microcosms* is a personal reading from the point of view of writers who live and participate in Latin American cultural life, as part of a collaborative effort between the writers, the museum professionals, the publishing houses Anagrama and Charco Press, and the Hay Festival. It moves into the public realm because it offers a reading of objects and collections created in this region, which form a part of its history but which have gone through reinterpretations and multiple shifts across time and space before they reached the British Museum, both as part of the book, published in Spanish and English, and also as part of the conversations about the whole experience taking place in the different Hay Festivals across the world. The encounter between the festival and the museum seeks to make visible these interpretations of history, culture and social and educational processes, both through the books and other forms of expression.

Each of the narrators uses language, that is to say their raw material, to take the pieces on unexpected journeys.

With their different styles and positions, the authors propose different uses of narrative time. So for example Juan Cárdenas transposes modern Western debates on creativity in relation to the functionality of art; Dolores Reyes withdraws her story from any specific timeframe; Yásnaya Elena A. Gil and Cristina Rivera Garza use futurism to criticise social and environmental realities of the present; while Velia Vidal and Joseph Zárate problematise the association between the museum and eternal conservation by reflecting on the impossibility of permanence. The sum of all these voices brings to light a new and necessary reflection on the relationship between Europe and America, addressing pivotal themes such as appropriation, spoliation, and identity. As is always the case with good literature there are no definitive answers: perhaps it only offers a route for exploring a landscape under construction. This book is rooted in the need to imagine, in the voices of ten Latin American authors, the voids that remain in the official discourse: retelling stories, through literature, about what we were, what we are and, perhaps, what we will be.

Cristina Fuentes La Roche OBE
International Director, Hay Festival

Dr. Laura Osorio Sunnucks
Santo Domingo Centre of Excellence for
Latin American Research, British Museum

Felipe Restrepo Pombo
Editor of the Spanish edition

*I*n this letter written in a post-apocalyptic future, Mejy describes the chance discovery of a yäjktstu'ujts (ceramic pot) washed up on the shores of Abya Yala (America) — a random remnant from an un-named colonial museum in the Northern Islands, a part of the world since destroyed by flooding. Gil's Indigenous futurism is inspired by a patojo from Tamazulapam del Espiritu Santo in the Mixe region of Oaxaca, Mexico, collected by Chloë Sayer and Elizabeth Carmichael in 1986. Although there are only very few ceramics from this area in the museum's collection, Sayer and Carmichael acquired over 4,000 local, popular, or Indigenous objects from Mexico in the late 1970s to mid-80s, many of which are associated with the Day of the Dead and were displayed in the 'Skeleton at the Feast' exhibition at the Museum of Mankind in 1991. While it was hoped that this kind of field collection would provide a contextual survey of the material culture associated with Mexican religion and everyday life, ironically, Gil focuses on the problematics of removing and so de-contextualising objects like the yäjktstu'ujts from the places they are made to be used. The difficulty of not activating this item in its community of origin and removing it in order to study and understand the past is echoed in Gil's imagined sustainable Indigenous future. In this new world, where the legitimating logics of the traditional museum are almost inscrutable, Gil uses temporal abstraction to consider present-day concerns about late-stage capitalism and coloniality.

Laura Osorio Sunnucks

LETTER TO A YOUNG MIXE HISTORIAN

Yásnaya Elena A. Gil

LETTER TO A YOUNG MIXE HISTORIAN

Yásnaya Elena A. Gil

Translated by Ellen Jones

Northern Commune,
the twenty-third day of the ninth month
of the year 2173

Dear Anaatuuj,
How are you? I imagine your work in the Mixe
community Historical Studies Society is keeping you
busy and you have not had time to write to me. I know it
isn't my turn in this old-school, nostalgic exchange we've
begun, but I'm writing anyway. I may not even end up
sending you these words, but I find it useful to imagine
a conversation with you, it allows me to get some of
my thoughts straight. I'm writing to you, then, because
there is something I've been worrying about. I've been
asked to write some reflections on historical work and

on my profession for the magazine published by the Global Coordinator of Historical Studies Societies. You will now understand my worry. I am very honoured to have been asked but also scared I will not be able to do the topic justice. What is the point of practising a profession like ours in this day and age? What advice can someone like me give, someone who has spent years managing the historical heritage of different global communities? These are the questions specified in the written invitation I received over a month ago now. I haven't managed to write much so far and that's why I'm turning to you. I know we haven't spoken a lot about our work in the Historical Studies Societies nor about the profession we now share; our relationship has been based mainly on doing day-to-day things together, along with your mother, and that has allowed us to hold onto a fondness for each other despite the distance. Perhaps this is a good moment, too, to tell you how proud I was the day I learned you had joined one of our societies. I imagine you now not only as my niece but also an interlocutor who, as though we were sharing a morning coffee, can guide me with her questions. Allow me to direct my words, then, to your imagined presence.

I found the question about the meaning of our work today a bit surprising, to be honest. I had never seriously asked myself that question. We know that, generally speaking, contemporary societies that survived the climate catastrophes caused by the period known as the Capitalist Night don't care much about the past — rather, we long to forget it. Far be it from me to defend that tragic period, from the nineteenth to the twenty-first century, when humanity refused to see reason and raced towards its own annihilation, destroying the natural world that was its home. I will not defend the pain that was caused, nor the countless deaths that occurred in that period before societies found a different way of existing on the land.

That said, when I fully joined the network of Historical Studies Societies, I was motivated by the possibility of doing a small amount of symbolic justice by managing the objects kept in those peculiar spaces known as museums, many of which have survived almost intact to this day. In order to achieve this project's objectives, I had to know all about that period, so despised today, so out of control and so irrational, in which the existence of museums was entirely unremarkable. After the climate collapse, when surviving societies had achieved a degree of equilibrium and stability, they began to wonder what to do with the museum objects that had survived. The work had been postponed for many decades and the question gone unanswered. But around that time, I learned that the project had been taken up again and that is why I decided to join the Historical Studies Societies and this project in particular. To achieve the initiative's objectives, we needed the collaboration of Societies all around the world. What should be done with the museum objects that had survived the climate catastrophe? What should be done with the objects belonging to a part of history we would rather forget?

To our current sensibility, museums feel like an aberration of memory. Just as zoos now seem to us inconceivable, to our minds museums are like prisons for memories. The way the Historical Societies work today leaves us in no doubt that history is a complex narrative ecosystem, which is why evidence of the past is kept in communal spaces that continually give each piece new meaning, rather than having it all bundled together in one place. It would seem absurd to us to confine everything valuable to a specific building miles away from the context in which it was created. Oral history is more important than ever for us, and objects are nothing but tools for activating our memories. Twentieth- and twenty-first-century museums seem to us the antithesis of our current practices of protecting history and memory, but that is in large part because we only have evidence of metropolitan museums from that period, which were erected as trophies of colonialism. Despite what has generally been assumed, at the height of the Capitalist Night there were communities who thought about history in more complex ways that did not simply serve the existing power structures. I won't spend time now discussing those communities, but I want to emphasise that our research has suggested that the great capitalist metropolitan museums were not the only ways of safeguarding and engaging with history and memory. We are preparing a piece on precisely this topic that is to be published shortly.

But back to the main point. As we know, the metropolitan museums were established as symbols of colonialist looting. While capitalism was devouring the natural landscapes of colonised territories around the world and hurling them at the market as commodities, museums were devouring objects belonging to their communities and turning them into museum objects. There was a kind of translation taking place, which may seem shocking to us today: an object that had a function – whether ritual, everyday, historical, or some other kind – in certain cultures, was ripped from its context and from the system that gave it meaning and turned into a museum object, to be exhibited alongside brief explanations in endless galleries where it was displayed for the public on a pedestal or in a glass case that prevented people from getting too close. The older it was, the more its value increased. And so the looting of the land was paralleled by the looting of items that were later confined to museums, orphans of a system that had once given them meaning, orphans of the communities that created and inherited them. I should say that this obsession with accumulating and classifying reached eyewatering levels. In particular, one of the most important museums in the now non-existent northern isles that were submerged in the great flood at the end of the twenty-first century, housed countless objects of different sizes that had been torn from communities and cultures subjugated by the colonising metropoles. The evidence we have today, and the research carried out by the Historical Studies Societies, suggests that, as colonialism expanded, this museum centre appropriated objects and evidence from each of the territories and communities that were conquered. At the time, the professions that most closely resembled our own were, unfortunately, often in the service of that extractivist spirit, which led, as we know all too well, to the great climate collapse.

There is much research still to be done, although there is currently little enthusiasm for delving further into that period. However, as I was going about my research, something unexpected happened that demonstrated to me the importance of our work. Before I describe how I came across a peculiar, inexplicably well-preserved museum object, allow me to give you some context. At the beginning of the twenty-first century, when capitalism and the colonial enterprise were firmly established, there were few territories left to conquer or subjugate. Metropolitan goods were available in almost every corner of the world and the Capitalist Night had darkened practically everything. By now it was rarely possible to satisfy a desire for the undiscovered exotic, and the empire's envoys, who had previously travelled the world, bringing back extraordinary historical samples from the most far-flung places, began to worry. When the sources of novelty no longer met the anxious desires of the disciplines of archaeology and anthropology, the seduction of the new had to come from somewhere else. Amid the absolute control exerted by the capitalist metropoles, there remained tiny islands of resistant communities organised into miniscule structures, which had avoided being swallowed up by the capitalist ocean. Back then, many of those communities were known as Indigenous peoples. Though it's hard to believe now, our community, the Mixe community, which used to be organised in much the same way as it is now, was among those considered Indigenous. Back then we had nothing like the recognition Mixe societies have today – it was a peripheral community in the middle of Abya Yala, which at the time was still known as America. Their existence on the periphery of the Capitalist Night motivated envoys from the great museum in the northern isles to turn to the lives of Indigenous peoples to try and satiate their need for exotic surprises. They sent people out, as far as possible from the metropoles, to collect things that, in their opinion, were worthy of safekeeping.

This context allowed me to understand a particular discovery that got me thinking about the importance of what we do. After extensive discussion, we decided that the surviving museum objects should, as far as possible, be returned to the present-day communities that are descended from the societies that produced them and from which they were taken. However, that task turned out to be more complicated than we originally thought. How could we establish which present-day societies were descended from which pre-climate collapse societies? The fact that only ten per cent of the estimated population at the beginning of the twenty-first century survived the climate catastrophes, along with the profound social reorganisation that gave rise to our current reality, compli-cated the work considerably. Many of the communities that had been considered peripheral during the Capitalist

Night were now centres of learning, working to achieve the much-desired environmental equilibrium that we were so close to achieving, while other communities had disappeared or had been reorganised under new hybrid identities. Each museum object that we endeavoured to return implied a challenge not only in terms of research but also in terms of how we decided which contemporary societies were to inherit it.

This was what we were working on when we received a series of boxes that had washed up on a beach near the seat of the Historical Studies Society to which I belong. After an initial inspection they decided to send them to our facilities. It was not especially unusual to learn that the remains of a so-called collection of the great museum in the northern isles had washed up on a beach. Without high expectations, I set about examining the contents, but then an object emerged from one of the boxes that left me speechless: it was a yäjktstu'ujts pot, not as shiny as they usually are when they're new, nor with that sheen they get after years of regular use. A yäjktstu'ujts is so familiar and commonplace a utensil among our communities that to pull one out of a box knowing it was housed in a museum during the Capitalist Night made me laugh in astonishment. Why would someone have wanted a yäjktstu'ujts as part of a museum collection? In the days that followed I examined its characteristics, trying as far as possible to put the absurd finding in context. Back then, in the eyes of the elites, a hand-made clay pot must have been considered strange, evidence of life outside the great metropoles where not only every utensil but even all the food had been through capitalist mass production. As characteristic as the shape of a yäjktstu'ujts pot is, it remains an everyday utensil that in our region is completely ordinary, as ordinary as the accepted truth that household goods should be created according to the principles of equilibrium with the land. The few items made outside of capitalist logic during the twentieth and twenty-first centuries must, back then, have satisfied that desperate desire for novelty, for the exotic. That is the only way I can explain to myself how a yäjktstu'ujts could have ended up as part of the collection in the great northern isles museum. No matter how carefully we examined its physical peculiarities and the information that accompanied it, we could find nothing extraordinary about the yäjktstu'ujts. Evidence was emerging before my eyes, direct from the past, that our community had inhabited the margins of capitalism and that yäjktstu'ujts, still so common in our everyday lives, were at one point turned into museum objects.

This absurd discovery allowed me to find meaning in my work among the Historical Studies Societies. My work involves returning objects extracted through processes of colonial violence to their own social systems of recognition, but it also involves keeping alive the memory of the excesses of the Capitalist Night, to ensure it is never repeated. That museum yäjktstu'ujts we found reminds us that capitalism did not encompass absolutely everything during that tragic period of history; that while the desires and imagination of the world were under the strictest control, small communities stood tall and resisted the logic of capitalist production. We must do justice by them and combat the now widely accepted idea that all societies behaved irrationally, threatening the planet and risking their own death by provoking the great environmental crisis. In the middle of that great darkness, small lights were resisting, safeguarding other ways of being human; unfortunately, many of them did not survive the great climate collapse that ensued. Others, like the Mixe community, were able to reform and to continue making the yäjktstu'ujts that, throughout those centuries of madness, were turned into museum objects. Remembering and talking about the societies that resisted late capitalism and colonialism has been the driving force behind my work in recent years.

Absurd as the situation might seem, we decided to take the yäjktstu'ujts to the Historical Studies Society in the Mixe region, despite the risk that our colleagues there would laugh at us. I set off, thrilled to be on my way to see your mother, who was pregnant with you at the time. After a long discussion, the object in question was taken to the Council of Mixe Assemblies, which decided that it should be given to the society of female clay workers, where it aroused very little curiosity. It didn't even compare to other old yäjktstu'ujts preserved in the kitchens of Mixe communities, which were made for preparing a particular kind of purple bean, tastiest when cooked slowly on a low heat. After listening to our story, an old woman told us it was an 'uncured' yäjktstu'ujts, which meant that in some sense it was new (by the way, it has always struck me as strange that in our language 'cure' is the word we use to describe the first time clay cooking utensils are soaked in hot atole to make sure they are properly sealed. I rather enjoy hearing the sound hot clay pots make when they are touched by the cornmeal drink. Don't you love that sound?) Almost two hundred years later, the yäjktstu'ujts that had once been a museum object had its first atole bath and thus began the life it would have had if the exoticising gaze had not confined it to a museum. Solely out of a sense of symbolic justice, I stayed in the society of female clay workers' community kitchen until the first beans were ready to eat. I live so far from my birthplace that I rarely get to eat those purple beans I miss so much (enjoy them while you can, in case life takes you to some far-off Historical Studies Society, as happened to me). I ate quietly alongside the clay workers while we talked about this and that, the fire crackling a few feet away and the yäjktstu'ujts sitting on the embers, returned to a system of values and symbolism that give it a purpose and a meaning, as familiar as they are necessary.

I know I have not quite managed to respond to all the questions I was asked in the letter of invitation, but now, having written to you, I believe I know where to begin my response. Thank you for your imagined presence. I have decided to send you this letter and I hope that, while it makes its way to you, I will finally be able to finish writing a coherent, publishable essay about my profession. Why study history after climate apocalypse?

See you soon, in harvest season.

Always,

Mejy

Gabriela Cabezón Cámara's interest in working with Wichí collections stems from a new political project she has embarked on that seeks to create awareness of the continuous displacement of Indigenous communities by capitalist enterprises in the Argentinian Chaco and the lack of response from the Argentinian state. When invited by the museum and Hay Festival to participate in this project, Cabezón Cámara was certain she wanted to work with the Wichí collections and integrate this research into her ongoing political project. During her first trip to the Chaco, she showed images of the collection to local communities, an approach that resonates with ethnographic research.

The label on the object she chose to work with reads 'Charms worn round the neck by men. Containing the roots and leaves which are for love, health, protection, fertility and guidance when lost. If a person is lost, the charm for guidance is opened, the powder sprinkled and the way is said to be found. These powders are made up by the medicine men only.' Rarely preserved with objects, this typewritten paper tag adopts a 'neutral' voice to classify this unassuming leather bracelet filled with powder from the Chaco. Collected in the 1930s by Alfred Cox during his three-year stay in the region as part of the Cambridge Mission, this object not only embodies Wichí beliefs at the time but also represents the painful and violent history of missionising that has defined spiritual life in the Argentinian Chaco until the present day. The items in Cox's collection are mostly from the Wichí (formerly known as Matacos, a derogatory term that is not an autonym, but is still present throughout academic literature) and their neighbours the Toba (or Qom). Gabriela's text describes her impressions of this first visit to the Wichí communities, demonstrating the effects of new evangelising narratives that demonise ancestral practices.

María Mercedes Martínez Milantchi

THE WICHÍ COMMUNITY

Gabriela Cabezón Cámara

THE WICHÍ COMMUNITY

Gabriela Cabezón Cámara

Translated by Carolina Orloff

'For dust you are, and to dust you shall return', affirms Genesis. If there's a place where that precept becomes omnipresent, it is here, in this esplanade of earth cracked open by the sun. We are barely sheltered by the mercy of a few carob trees, their dark trunks, their tiny leaves in clusters of tender green, their naked and contorted branches. The carob trees that are still here give us shelter with their caring, vital shade. Not many remain, and yet everything gets organised around them: from the small houses in this settlement – which used to be nomadic until it was cornered – to the meals, the mate drinking, the assemblies. Almost everything is communal. Even the water tap, even the toilets. And the kitchen, underneath the carob tree: a few logs on the dusty ground, a metal rack over the logs, a huge pan over the rack. The table on which the ingredients for the stew lay: rice, pasta, the few vegetables that can be found – the soil is pitiful windblown dust and the water is saline – and chicken. We are in charge of buying the chicken. Here, in the Wichí community of Altos de la Sierra, on the border between Argentina and Bolivia, everyone wants to eat chicken. So, my friend Natalia Brizuela and myself, feeling wealthy for the first time in our lives, hop in the car and go to buy chickens. We are around thirty people coming together to eat, maybe more. Almost every woman is a mother here. They come and go with their long colourful skirts, their bright almond-shaped eyes, their stunning dark heads of hair. And the children in their arms or running around them. And the dogs, skinny but loved. Things are brought over: cutlery, plates, cups, chairs. We are well looked after. They bring us buckets of water for our room house. With infinite patience, they explain to us how to come and go. We chat. The conversation is a texture that gets woven all day long, like a net that brings us together stitch by stitch and contains us. All the conversations are the weaving of multiple voices.

'And before? What did your parents used to eat? Your grandmothers?'

'They ate corzuela.'

'And what happened?'

'There's none left.'

'What else did they eat?'

'Mistol, my granny used to cook it well.'

'But there is none left.'

'Surí.'

'It's forbidden.'

'Mulita, armadillo.'

'There's none left.'

There's none left.

What there is plenty of is disbelief and sadness, long-lasting. What there is plenty of is stupor and grief because there is none left of most things. The herbs that the grandmothers used for healing, are also gone.

'There are some still here.'

'Very few.'

'Besides, hardly anyone knows how to do it any more. María knows.'

'Will you be teaching the young ones, María?'

'You have to go deep into the forest.'

'Us women go deep into the forest.'

'But the forest seems to be getting further and further away.'

'We go where we've always gone, and now it's barbed-wired.'

'We have to ask for permission to go in.'

'It's fenced with barbed wire.'

'If we don't ask for permission from the owners, perhaps we get shot, we get shot with a rifle.'

'It's fenced with barbed wire.'

It's fenced with barbed wire.

What's left of the forest is under new ownership. The Wichí people have been living here for centuries. But now, the *here* is almost dead, chopped down, burnt, bulldozed over, turned into fields to grow soya or to raise cattle. It is fenced. The voices overlap. Softly, delicately. The Wichí women do not raise their voices, they don't judge, impose themselves. They think before they speak. Then they translate into the language of clearing, of barbed wire, of hunger and thirst. They translate into our language, Spanish. *Español* they call it now in Spain instead of *castellano*, as if to register it as their trademark. There is no need: the mark is indelible. Round here you feel it

23

on your skin. The language of extinction. The language of Spain and of the Argentine State. As I was saying, the voices talk over each other softly, delicately. And they burst into a choral work: there's nothing left, they say together immersed in their astonishment, it is barbed-wired, they say together immersed in their pain. And the dust and the over forty-degree heat and the hunger that today at least does not hurt. Today this hunger is joyful: today there is food on the table. The conversation continues to unfold and I lose track of how much we understand each other and how much we don't, because they are translating from their own language, and from their shattered world. But oh, it is all still so beautiful, their world is still so alive. Like ours, but different.

'Oh' because this shattered world is life that is suffering, and is dying for shameful reasons. Lack of food, for instance. Lack of drinkable water. Lack of medicines. Everything that used to make up a world is now missing, and that world has been crushed.

'They've forgotten about us.' On the picket line, this is what the Wichís say: this is the cradle of this form of protest. People get together and light a fire in the middle of the road. They don't let anyone through. This, here, means long conversations. The Wichí people believe in conversations. They also believe that the State, founda-tions, NGOs and universities should send resources to their communities. But it's always to the other ones. Someone always makes them believe that there are people benefitting, and that those people are not them. But no one is benefitting. We are going to spend several hours completing a journey that should take only one. We are going to talk to people in three communities. We are going to see roofs blown away in the last storm and replaced by tarpaulins. We are going to be told that there is no nurse and no doctor in the local clinic. That there are no longer trees yielding fruit. That there are dead fish floating down the river. That they want them to leave their land. That bees are dying and there is no honey left. That planes fumigate from the sky, killing their animals and whatever they had managed to grow in their garden. That their children are falling sick.

They've forgotten about us.

During the whole journey up here, 1,600 kilometres from Buenos Aires, we felt like we were passing through a moribund landscape. The West, that inhumane and foul factory that reproduces itself and kills everything else, seems to be the absolute winner. With its new owners, its 'there is no more', its barbed wire. So different are these owners compared to the previous ones. Because the land always had owners. The weavers tell us about this. They don't just weave conversations; they also weave art. They don't like the word art. They prefer craft instead. It doesn't matter that we explain to them that for us, their customers, those who speak the language of there is no more, the language of barbed wire and hunger, that to us art is better, we pay more for it. They weave, they are weavers. In order to weave, they have to go into the forest. The forest is further and further away. And it's behind barbed wire. Yet, there is still the cháguar, *Bromelia hieronymi* in that other imperial language used by botanists in the past. Not much, and behind barbed wire, but there's still some.

'We have to travel about fifteen kilometres to find cháguar.'

'We go on our bikes.'

'We also walk.'

'Our husbands give us a ride on their motorbikes.'

'And Melania too, she knows how to ride a motorbike!'

'We have to ask the owner for permission to get in.'

They talk about the previous owner, the one that was there since forever. The spirit of the forest, the one that looks after it. The owner does not allow them to take much: the owner has rules to allow the Wichís to live and also rules for the forest. For eating, for basic use – the owner allows them to take enough for that. If someone takes more than they are supposed to, if someone does not respect this, they get punished. Their lives are turned into a nightmare. We are told everything, our bodies in a circle, the fire in the middle, surrounded by carob trees, surrounded by something which we cannot quite define but which we can certainly feel. Perhaps it's the weaving of community, the owner of all things Wichí.

'The forest is dangerous.'

'You can't always go and get what you need.'

'When we are roaming the forest and birds like the fwitsanii or the wilswuk turn up, with their long beaks, it means we need to leave. It's dangerous. If they don't want us to, we can't take from it.'

'When we can take, we peel the leaves of the cháguar there and then. Like this, look: we remove the part that sits on top and the one from underneath, and the part that we keep is this one, you see? The middle part.'

The cháguar is a plant with long leaves and spiky edges and a sharp tip. They grow in rosettes and form clumps on the rocks, sometimes they are silver in colour, sometimes dark green. It pricks you: the cháguar is a plant that can hurt. It defends itself. So in order to harvest it, they use sharp sticks. Plant by plant. They stay overnight, they sleep in the forest to continue harvesting. In the forest, listening to the breathing of the trees, of the animals that still remain. The sky above them, strafed with stars: they still haven't taken that away from them. I imagine these women, under the starry skies, speaking 'the tongue' – as they call it – sharing their problems, their ambitions. Some they shared with us: to graduate from secondary school, to study, to own a sewing machine and a long black gala dress with a slit on one side, to recover their land, that their children don't have to leave when they grow older, to drive a van, to own a van, to have access to water always, to have access to food always, to keep warm in winter, to be able to send their children to university, to have access to land, to learn from their grandparents the powers of herbs; to see the forest grow back. For moments, here – where it is possible to be because there are trees (the sun and heat are wounding where there aren't any) – the threads of conversation fade away: the birds sing loudly and they talk happily about their work, this wonderful art they create with their hands and the cháguar: everything seems possible. Until they get back at least part of their land, and stop the killing, the killing of the forest. Until they tear down the barbed wire. Let the previous owners return. Let the trees return and let the birds burst open the air singing their songs willy-nilly. The silence that exists where there used to be a forest and now there is only wasteland, is deafening.

'And then we do this, with our fingers and our nails, and we take the pulp from each leaf.'

'We wash them with water and leave them to dry in the sun for two days.'

'Once they are dry, the fibres are all lovely and white.'

'Then we dye them, using roots.'

'And ashes.'

'Each root is a colour.'

'To get yellow, we dye it with fat from the lizard.'

'Lizard... the animal?'

'No, no, it's a type of root.'

'Once it's been dyed, we do what we want to do.'

What they do when they do what they want is of

an extraordinary beauty. Objects that smell of the forest and glow in their woven splendour. Objects that you can appreciate with your nose, your skin and your eyes. Yicas, backpacks, purses, handbags. And huge shawls that explode with colours; they are abstract in their design even when they have some figurative details. Lysergic explosions full of life. Contrasts, frictions and tensions that make us quiver. Checkerboards, mermaids, diamonds, uninterrupted lines that go up and down like snakes trained to slither in straight lines. Gigantic maps of a foreign territory. These objects and works are excessive. They exceed all frames of reference, because they were not conceived for our world. What should the market price be of, say, a handbag made entirely by hand, from the gathering of the plant with which is made to the very thread with which it's woven? What is the price of an object that never takes less than ten days to make? How does this economy of the gift fit into the parameters of capitalism? It fits in by losing out: not just because up until very recently these extraordinary objects were paid for with flour, yerba or sugar, and then resold at a huge profit. But rather because they were conceived for a different world. Traditionally these pieces were created as objects to be used, not to be traded. The yica is the object you take with you when going fishing or gathering fruit, it was not born out of a calculation of profit. The yica comes with you as a kind of tie, as part of the weave that ties you to your community.

Big names and big institutions. Still, they don't always have food on their plates. Let alone water. Every morning and every afternoon, they sweep the social space in their houses: the exterior esplanade of dust. Have you ever seen women sweeping dust floors until they are clean? Can you comprehend how long it takes to settle the dust? And for how long do you think dust agrees to be still? And every morning, and afternoon, every noon and every evening, they go with their buckets to get water from the single communal tap.

In Santa Victoria Este, a poor city raised on top of the dust on the banks of the Pilcomayo river, none of that, neither the institutions nor the world of art as a commodity, is visible, despite the fact that we are at an art exhibition. There is no champagne or fancy clothes, either. People are drinking soft drinks and some traditional snacks, as well as mass-produced biscuits. The heat is hard to bear. We praise and celebrate, we buy as much as we can afford. If I could, I'd buy it all: it is so gorgeous, so full of life. But enough shopping: the women are about to talk. Shyly. They are embarrassed to speak in public and to speak in Spanish. But they go ahead, and they say:

'In the Wichí language there is a word, *notechel*, which means ancestral. There is another word that is *ta otakie*, meaning future, or rather, forward. Our work combines these two words: it is something that takes the ancestral forward.'

I wonder if this moribund world is perhaps beginning to be born again?

Taking the ancestral forward. What is art if not precisely that? Among us – the semi-Western and the full-on Western – there exists the category of the author. The merchandise that is the individual figure of the author, that which remains out of the fraudulent concept of genius. That's not the case here. Here it's about all of them, even when it's also about them individually. Each one of them can exist because they are a unity of all of them together. They try to explain this to me, and this time I think I get it.

We are about to leave. It's the third time that we look at the photos together showing some pieces belonging to the Wichí community in the hands of the British

29

Museum. There is one that they identify at once: it's a leather bracelet that incorporates, in a circular form – as with everything that has to do with the idea of coming together in this community – a number of tiny bags also made of leather, filled with seeds. The women laugh and make jokes (I think) in their tongue. Their cacique walks by and they call him over. We tell him that the British Museum has this piece which belongs to them.

'Let them keep it. That object is to win false love. It's evil.'

'But didn't your grandparents used to wear it?'

'Yes, they did.'

'And your grandparents were evil?'

'Yes. They didn't know Our Lord. They were under the spell of the devil. That's why they were exploited.'

They explain to me that this bracelet is witchcraft. They don't say it to me explicitly, but I deduce that it is circular and it has the tiny bags arranged in the same way that they arrange their bodies when they come together. Because this bracelet fosters encounters: its purpose is to attract human and non-human animals. For hunting and for loving. What the women find hilarious is the part about the human animals, the part about false love. Old men use it to seduce young girls, they say, but the spell does not last for more than two days.

'But that's not love. True love needs work, true love needs to be built. That in the image belongs to the devil.'

On that, we agree with the cacique. We don't argue about the other question, the issue that sticks out like a sore thumb: now that they are with Our Lord, they are being exploited all the same. Mercilessly.

'And what do you make of the fact that the British have things that belong to your people and you don't have anything that belongs to them?'

'They can keep the things. What we need here are

scholarships for kids to study. We need lawyers, doctors…
That's what we need.'

Will the British Museum listen to these Anglican
Wichís? Will someone tell the Queen that the most
distant of her faithful need some of what was stolen to
be returned to them? Their spiritual world, even, stigma-
tised as diabolical by those Anglicans who were at once
scourge and shelter. Come on, Queen, come on, British
Museum. These people have been robbed even of their
own religion! And also a huge part of the Chaqueño
forest: 'La Forestal' was the name of the British company
that did it. It was not the only one, but it was one of the
greatest destroyers of this territory. They need scholarships. Doctors, lawyers. Subsidies to dig wells and extract
drinking water. A great exhibition of their contemporary
art. Just let us know: they're waiting for you, right here.

Only 40 of the 590 ceramic objects in the Moche collection are exhibited at the British Museum. The piece chosen by Juan Cárdenas does not have this good 'fortune'. As part of one of the largest bodies of pre-Columbian art in the British Museum's collection, this ceramic reveals an extended practice of pottery used as a complex mode of communication which exceeded simple repetition. This object dates from the years 200-850 CE and comes from the northern coast of what is now known as Peru. It was donated in 1882 by the archaeologist and member of the Cambridge Antiquarian Society, Walter K. Foster. The figure depicts corn, one of the staple foods in the Moche economy, embodied in three deities. In the Moche world, its cultivation was so sophisticated that two harvests per year were achieved; it was not only a fundamental source of food but also the main ingredient for chicha, a ritual beverage popular among Andean societies.

Who moulded this piece? What was she or he thinking when it was created? Arguably, disciplinary limits narrow the imagination surrounding museum objects, so this fictional entry into a potter's mind by Cárdenas is an opportunity to rethink the artefact within its creative context. The historical-scientific aspect takes a back seat, and the author takes an imagined, personal, and emotional approach. The writer challenges the archaeological conception of pottery as part of a political-religious system and a platform for the dissemination of collective ideas. Instead, he mobilises the concept of radicality within a creative space, in which the imagined potter aims to change the course of tradition with original ideas. Cárdenas invites us to immerse ourselves in the personal space of rebellion amid a climatic and political crisis. By implying a parallel with current affairs, he links the experience of a Moche creator to that of the reader.

Magdalena Araus Sieber

EXTRACT FROM THE DIARY OF A JOURNEY ALONG THE NORTH COAST OF PERU

Juan Cárdenas

EXTRACT FROM THE DIARY OF A JOURNEY ALONG THE NORTH COAST OF PERU

Juan Cárdenas

Translated by Christina MacSweeney

19 June, 2018

In the evening, sitting on the terrace of the hotel in Huanchaco where I've been staying for the past week, I decide to browse some articles about the Moche culture. A quick Google search has me washing up on the website of the British Museum, whose collection includes quite a few Moche pieces, ranging from musical instruments and knitting needles to the well-known and greatly admired ceramic heads, unique of their kind in the whole of pre-Columbian art for their supremely realistic representations of the human face. It isn't clear if the heads – almost all made on a scale between 1:3 and 1:5 – were moulded in a similar tradition to that of Western portraiture as there's also speculation about their possible ceremonial, votive or even medical uses; that last theory may contain a glimmer of truth, given the large number of heads of this type representing illnesses and congenital deformities. In other words, did Moche doctors utilise these heads to keep a morphological record of illnesses in the hope of improving their diagnoses or documenting symptoms? Or was it in fact the priests who had recourse to these almost perfect figures, in which the individual features of each face are, to say the least, striking, in order to gain the favour of the gods and so guarantee the cure or social status of the person who served as the model?

While I look at the images in the British Museum's collection, I become lost in idle speculation. All at once, I'm almost effortlessly capable of imagining a young Moche artist at a moment when his civilisation is in sharp decline. He's working in a pottery alongside fifty or sixty others, who carry out to the letter the orders arriving from the various ecclesiastic or political sectors. That is to say, it is their task to keep alive the imagery, the symbols of power. It would be no exaggeration to say that the efficacy of the gods within every aspect of Moche social order depends on that small number of artists. But for their untiring labour, their dedication to these images that make divine powers palpable and transform all the abstract forces that govern the lives of men into recognisable figures (seabirds, waves, reed boats, crabs, spiders etc.), it is quite likely that the empire would have collapsed decades before. The whole Moche ideological structure, the very basis of its economy, rests to a large extent on the shoulders of its potters. The person who, not without a touch of horror, finds himself thinking these thoughts is our young artist, who has been working for hours on a receptacle representing the god of maize, a god that is three gods in one or the three bodies of one god fused in a great corncob. The three identical heads are baring their teeth in the manner of all agrarian gods, who demand the payment of tribute in human blood. The young artist knows the figure well as he's modelled it in clay many times and even has a dozen moulds that could save him much of the work, but this time a vague sense of fury is urging him to create something different. Something that, in effect, breaks the mould. The city states, almost all melting away under the extreme climatic conditions, are at that time experiencing a veritable crisis of faith and rumours are rife about the waning powers of some of the gods, in particular those controlling food production. In recent times, the priestly caste has decided to triple the number of human sacrifices, but nothing seems to satisfy the gods. Among his colleagues in the workshop, there are several potters who secretly argue and whisper. You can't have it both ways, they say, either the gods are ignoring us because we're doing something wrong or they are losing their authority, their potency. Maybe our gods have already been defeated by other, much more powerful ones. New gods are replacing them. Such heresies are circulating not only in the workshop but throughout the city. Our young artist tries to ignore them. Despite the fact that the crisis has extended over many decades and the situation has only got worse, he wants to believe in the supreme order of the universe that he has been taught since his childhood, an order that, incidentally, underlies the ultimate meaning of his work as an artist. Art is, fundamentally, a labour that is indistinguishable from political proselytism. It's the reinvigorating slogan that renews our faith in the system, the image that tricks our senses into making shock and conformity coincide in a single movement of the spirit. Our young artist, nonetheless, isn't the kind of naive fellow who tries to bury his head in the sand. There is no denying the crisis; the empire is literally crumbling before the eyes of its subjects. But that is not the fault of the gods or the teachings of the priestly caste, which for centuries has provided ample evidence of its wisdom and good governance. We must lay the responsibility on ourselves, he thinks, on ourselves as artists. Isn't it true that there has been practically no variation in the iconography over the last seven or eight centuries? Haven't we been mechanically repeating identical forms for many generations? Why are we so determined to continue using these same old moulds? Why does our art – with its excellence of technique and sophistication of form and themes – feel so stagnant? To put it another way, if the life ordained by the gods is one of movement and perpetual change, if what we observe in the world of the agrarian and marine gods is a series of forces in constant transformation, why shouldn't our art do justice to those forces? Why does our art insist on paralysis when the world is crying out for us to show ourselves capable of change? Why do we go on using these moulds when we should be creating new forms? All those questions swirl around and pile up as the young artist works his material. A new image of the god of maize emerges directly from his hands. A devout image, born of the most profound confidence in the religion that determines Moche daily life down to the last detail. The priests – and the workshop masters who carry out their orders – tend to be very strict in their evaluation of how the gods should be represented. The young artist knows, therefore, that these demonstrations of creative fervour may be frowned on by his superiors, so rigorous in their application of the iconography of the pantheon. Some malicious spirit might accuse him of heresy, but at the same time it's clear to him that the climate crisis, the cyclical uprisings of the fishermen no longer ready to follow orders without question, the epidemics, the physical deterioration of the administrative buildings and temples; in short, the prolonged social discontent is in some way a justification of this iconoclastic impulse. What gradually appears between his skilled hands is, without doubt, perfectly recognisable as the old god of maize, but there is something in the body, in the fused bodies that are also corncobs merging together, something in the figure that makes one think of a field devastated by rain. Not a field of healthy maize swaying in the summer breeze, but a heap of mud, grains and husks, the harvest in the quagmire caused by overflowing canals. It is a representation of the triple god of maize that faces up to the crisis within the empire and somehow manages to incorporate – in the literal sense – the ruin of the whole system in the figure of one of the most important gods in the pantheon. The young potter has put his art at the service of the official political system and religion and is satisfied with his work, all the more so when his superiors take note of his creation. It's a small vessel for drinking the sacred chicha, the youth explains, worthy of use by a high priest in the most sacred rituals. A small huddle of curious onlookers forms around him and, after much discussion, there is still no agreement about the appropriacy of the figure. Some consider it scandalous and demand it be destroyed before any member of the priestly caste can see it. Others, more daring in their outlook, proclaim a radical change in the canons of the representation of the gods and their prowess. The young artist attempts to defend his piece with pious arguments in keeping with the doctrine, but his words fall on deaf ears because the figure has already provoked such controversy. The god of maize himself inspired me, he finally says in desperation, the god of maize in person has ascended from the depths of the earth to suggest this form to me. I might disobey our artisanal canons, but disobeying a god is something I'd never dare to do. All I've done is instil in the clay what the god himself has asked of me. The polemic soon reaches the ears of the military-priests, but they can come to no conclusion either. They are the typical avatars of official art in an era of civilisation collapse. There are times when an excess of piety impels forms towards heresy, towards the final dismantling of the ideology that sustains everything. At others, revolutionary zeal, the promise of emancipation that finds a home in the heart of all great art, is barely able to breathe a little life into the most decadent apparatus of the society in crisis. No one is capable of foreseeing the effects of a signifying object, much less one that is alleged to have been created at the dictates of a god. In any case, it is never easy to trace a clear line between official and revolutionary art. There is only one point on which they are in agreement, both in the workshop and among the religious sectors: the piece created by the young potter is lovely. That is to say, it is capable of transmitting consolation, beauty and serenity, while still retaining its terrifying nature as a god who, with each passing day, demands more and more sacrifices.

The British Museum website doesn't give much information about this formidable ceramic piece. It simply says 'pot.' The date of acquisition is 1882 and there is absolutely no trace of how the object came to be in the museum. But it isn't too difficult to imagine the circumstances: tomb robbers, an English traveller working for some colonial enterprise (Rubber? Railways? Banks?), a long chain of intermediaries, a buyer from the museum acquiring the piece as part of a large lot of antiquities and fetishes from South America. These stories tend to follow a pattern.

So, the fact that museums of the former colonial metropolises store these types of pieces in a somewhat isolated manner – that is to say, without historical context or greater detail of their acquisition, much less their excavation – hinders the reconstruction of their meanings and specific uses. And that is why local archaeologists working in this area claim the objects are spoiled – *se malogran*, as they say in Peru – when they are taken from the places where they were buried and treated as if they did not belong to a complex mesh of objects. Yet the mesh is exactly what matters to those archaeologists. Not the individual pieces, but what they say to us when we find them within a given constellation of meaning determined by the location in which they were uncovered.

Museums of former colonial metropolises – and the British Museum is possibly the paradigm of this type of institution – are concerned with preserving each individual object, particularly when the pieces come from the ancient cultures of the Global South. However, the price science pays for this style of conservation is very high: there's no doubt that the object in question is in a safe place, under the jealous care of experts, but during this process the very story behind it is lost. Such pieces become mute when they are separated from the others surrounding them in their burial places. Or at least, they stop speaking and are irreversibly divorced from what their creators attempted to say when they placed them there. Who now knows what the true use of this figure was, the meaning and intention behind the creation of the triple god of maize, with its three heads and long fangs? Given the circumstances, our only option is to fantasise irresponsibly and dream ourselves there, in that lost world, which is also our world. Our lost world.

Based at Cambridge University, Carlos Fonseca was able to visit the museum's collections in person. Fonseca was interested in the people behind the collecting, explorers and their early collecting practices that included both organic and cultural materials. Although he only spent half a day in the storage facility, his interests drew him to the figure of Sir Robert Schomburgk and kanaimà, a practice of ritual death from the highlands of Guyana. Sir Robert Hermann Schomburgk was a German explorer specialising in botany and geography. Sent on an expedition by the British Government (1835-1839) to former British Guiana, Schomburgk famously described the existence of a giant water lily he named Victoria regia. He also gave a significant ethnographic collection made up of over 50 objects from Guyana to the British Museum in 1836. Many of these have never been on display.

The term kanaimà refers to both the practitioners and the practice itself, which consists of slow torture that aims to completely disorient the victim. Although kanaimà is a millenary practice of unknown age, it took on a different valence when borders were being drawn by Europeans in the 1800s. Although this practice is not related to any particular items in the collection, curator Laura Osorio described it in vivid detail during Fonseca's visit. She emphasised that kanaimà is said to have gained presence with the encroaching effects of colonialism, at a moment when Indigenous communities were displaced from their lands and forced into smaller areas leading to the intensification of inter-tribal warfare. Fonseca recognises his positionality in the piece by intertwining references to his Costa Rican familial ties and his experience in the museum stores with the details of an imagined past lived by Schomburgk.

María Mercedes Martínez Milantchi

HERITAGE

Carlos Fonseca

HERITAGE

Carlos Fonseca

Translated by Frank Wynne

I have gathered a garland of other men's flowers, and nothing is mine but the cord that binds them.
Montaigne

A *simple tale of revenge*, Isabel had said, unable to conceive that, first and foremost, it had been about flowers. Enormous flowers that floated languorously on waters that always reminded me of the heavens, I would see them on the Sunday afternoons when we visited grandfather in the mountains. After my grandmother's death, the old man had hidden himself away from the world, his silence shared only with these flowers which he painted obsessively, as though attempting to become a Monet of the tropics. No one said anything. We would watch as he finished one painting and, the following week, when we came back, would find him working on another.

Some men collect coins; others collect stamps. My grandfather collected paintings of immense water lilies. On those afternoons, fearful of interrupting him, I would creep into his studio and stare from afar at the white petals unfurling above leaves so huge that, according to my father, a baby could float on them.

It took some time before I understood where he had come by this strange fascination. But, one afternoon, after putting away his oil paints, I saw him go over to what looked like a sprig of flowers. In fact, it was some sort of feathered crown or headdress.

'Take it, it's a gift. It belonged to my father.'

'The Brazilian?' I said, with the wariness of those broaching a subject about which they know absolutely nothing.

'Yes, him.'

Not wanting to upset him, since I know that his relationship with his father had been a difficult one, I thanked him for the gesture, thinking about the rumours that circulated in the family about this man whom we had nicknamed *the Brazilian*, for the simple reason that we were loath to use his other names: the smuggler, the deserter, the liar. Abraham Fonseca: we knew his name only through the contours of his absence. He had committed some terrible crime at a very young age and since then, disappeared every year and spent long periods on the highways and byways of the south, professing to be smuggling. No one believed him, and there were rumours that he spent his time holed up in villages along the coast where he had a handful of other families to feed.

Which is why, that afternoon, I was surprised to be given the headdress, and even more surprised to hear my grandfather recount the story of how his father, on one of his sorties in the south, had encountered an evangelical missionary who had sold him this headdress, on whose ancient leather thong was inscribed the legend: 'Sororeng, interpreter to Robert Schomburgk, Guiana, 1840.'

'It was his only legacy to me,' he said.

'But where is Guyana, grandfather?'

'In the far south, where men go to lose themselves,' he said angrily.

I was mesmerised by this phrase. That night, when I got home, I took down one of the encyclopaedias that no one ever leafed through and searched the entries until I found one that devoted a couple of lines to this place about which I knew almost nothing. There it was, on a map that situated it between countries that I could place. Then, I thumbed the pages until I came upon an entry that mentioned the German who name was inscribed on the leather strap. From what I read, in the middle of the last century, Robert Schomburgk had been sent by the Royal Geographical Society on a voyage of discovery to the new colonies of the British Empire.

He was set a double task: to find the fabled land of El Dorado which Sir Walter Raleigh believed he had glimpsed in the Orinoco basin, and to demarcate the border between Guiana and Brazil. He did not succeed in discovering the idyllic Lake Parime promised by the English explorer, but just when he began to fear that his voyage would be a failure, he stumbled upon an utterly unexpected discovery: on the waters of the Berbice river, on a placid inlet where he had ventured by mistake, he saw the unfurling buds of a species never seen before. The leaves, almost two metres in diameter, floated lazily on the waters, like some chimera in the midst of the jungle. *Victoria regia* was the short name given by British botanists to these gigantic water lilies, in honour of the new queen.

I remember that, after reading the story of the discovery of this flower of Empire that night, I spent little time thinking about England. For me, who had never set foot outside Costa Rica, it was the mention of Guyana, this *terra incognita* in the heart of Latin America which fuelled my fantasy, epitomised by that strange name – *Sororeng* – about which I could find nothing in the encyclopaedia, but whose very obscurity fired my imagination. It was then that I sensed that the flowers my grandfather painted on Sundays were his private way of reclaiming the father who had vanished amid the mirages of the south.

Perhaps this is why, though almost three decades have passed since those childhood afternoons, as I listen to the curator recount the odyssey of the solitary Sororeng, who acted as interpreter for Schomburgk on his southern voyages, I find myself distractedly thinking about grandfather's flowers. *El viejo* could never have imagined that I would one day find myself standing in front of cabinets filled with the wonders Schomburgk first donated to the British Museum on his return from Guyana in 1939. Before me on the shelves, the pieces from the collection trace the images that Isabel is describing.

While she takes out hammocks and headdresses, arrows and flutes, ceremonial robes and sonorous instruments, I picture them as they would surely have been seen in the winter of 1840 by the English people who struggled through the chill pea-souper to reach the building housing The Guiana Exhibition. I can see them as though on a stage: in the centre, anxiously pacing because of the poor attendance, the diminutive, beardless Schomburgk with those ringlet curls that, even in his thirties, make him look like a child. Next to him, some ten years younger but two times heavier, Saramang, the indigenous Macushi who has travelled with the German since his first excursions, is smiling as he fastens a bag while, behind him, Corrienau, the Warao man recruited on the last voyage, is complaining of the cold. Then I think I spot Sororeng, more distant and more withdrawn than the others, more conscious, perhaps, of the preposterousness of the venture that has brought them here.

At the time, he would be thirty-five, the same age as Schomburgk, but his face is marked by the wisdom of those who know that something has come to an end and all that remains is to endure. A year earlier, while exploring the borderlands of Guyana, Schomburgk happened on a village that had been reduced to rubble. During a slave raid, the last remaining Parvilhana villages had been razed to the ground, and among the ashes the explorer had encountered newly enslaved indigenous peoples who had pleaded with him for help. Unable to offer assistance, since he could not determine whether they lived in British or Brazilian territory, and whether he had the legal power to intervene, Schomburgk could do nothing but carry on downriver. It was there, in a small cave, that he discovered Sororeng, hiding with his family. He was surprised to hear the man speak English, in the hoarse, measured, taciturn voice which he would later use as his interpreter, and which he would use, years later, to speak with all those who dared to see him, not merely as a curious exhibit on display, but for what he was: a man. A man cast out by history, one of the frontier people who fought for survival amid slavery, colonialism, nationalism and evangelism.

While Isabel unpacks the boxes, I feel like I can see them all — this little quartet whom Schomburgk, not without a certain paternalism, always referred to as 'my Indian family', but mostly I see him, Sororeng, lost among the stuffed animals and the exotic plants that threaten to turn everything into a puerile cosmorama, since it was ridiculous to imagine that this colonial exhibition would succeed, as Schomburgk hoped, in kindling a political awareness among the spectators. I picture this scene, and I think about my grandfather: the old man who had never left Costa Rica, claimed that he had everything he needed in the mountains, yet had given me the one thing that, in time, had brought me to this place.

On the display table, the headdress shares the space with the various other objects from the collection, as though finally reunited with a family from which it has long been estranged. For years, while following in the footsteps of *the Brazilian*, travelling and crossing borders, I took the headdress with me as though it were keeping alive the link to its absent family. Around this solitary item, I try to fashion a private museum: one that safeguards the memories of my grandfather and the fantasies built up around my great-grandfather.

Now, as I listen to Isabel recount the story of Sororeng, I begin to understand that, in its nomadic peregrinations, the headdress was merely following in the footsteps of its owner. 'My Indian family' was how Schomburgk referred to the group of natives who travelled with him to London in the winter of 1840, words that could only half-hide his irony: the only thing that seemed to connect them was their alien status and their loneliness. They lodged in a small flat in the heart of Soho, and those who saw them emerge from the doorway of 19 Golden Square could not imagine what united this strange group made up of a

Macushi, a Warao, a Parvilhana and a German.

Little did they suspect that the expedition that connected them was the one the related the origin of the flower of empire, which Schomburgk had attempted to restage in The Guiana Exhibition, but whose splendour had been overshadowed by the absence of one thing: the flower itself. No matter that Schomburgk filled the stage with dahlias, begonias, petunias, camellias and orchids in countless 'Wardian cases', no matter that Sororeng, Saramang and Corrienau wandered about amid animal hides and curious reptiles, the spectators felt the absence of the very thing that had brought them here: nowhere in the exhibition was there any sign of *Victoria regia*.

Because The Guiana Exhibition of 1840 masked a sad fact: Schomburgk had glimpsed the flower only once. Just as Raleigh had only briefly espied Lake Parime on the Rupununi savannah, so the flower that now entranced the imperial imagination had disappeared in the dry season that followed the rains. Schomburgk had had time only to make a sketch of the floral wonder he claimed to have seen: the huge circular leaves spanning more the two metres; the magnificent flower, a perfect commingling of white and purple, and the sharp-thorned stem that commanded respect. Enough to kindle the spirit of a public eager for news and for glory.

That same summer, following the death of William IV, a young princess had ascended the throne and the German cunningly suggested naming the flower in honour of the youthful queen. *Victoria regia:* a fine name for a flower, and for a queen, a fine headline for a magazine. Little did the British imagine that, while journalists were spreading rumours of the matchless flower, Schomburgk was vainly struggling to find it again. Elusive as a mirage, the flower had been tracked down by two explorers, but all attempts to replant it had failed.

The English public who followed the paths of curiosity that winter to visit the exhibition were met by disappointment: only a painting of the flower adorned the walls of the exhibition hall; there was no sign of the plant itself. Not a seed, not a stem, not so much as a wilted bud. Nothing but three natives around whom Schomburgk paced nervously, pontificating on the precarious plight of aboriginal peoples in the colonies, not realising that, without intending to, he had recreated the cruelties of human zoos.

There are no photographs of the exhibition, Isabel told me, but that did not matter.

I needed only her words to imagine the sadness of Sororeng, the bafflement he must have felt seeing himself here, forced to take the place of a flower that refused to appear. How could one relocate the tropics? How could one transport the fantasy without it being diluted in the process? This was the question the Victorians were beginning to ask themselves at the time. I remember that, as a child, I always loved terrariums, Wardian cases and glass aquariums, microcosms that seemed to contain a world in miniature, a private realm of the plants and animals that lived there. My grandfather had become something of the kind, a man who had stubbornly retreated to his own Wardian case, his vivarium replete with flowers, the studio from which we only ever saw him emerge at nightfall. A man immersed in a private world, whose gestures, unbeknownst to him, echoed the solitary figure of Sororeng, more than a century earlier, framed against chill English sunsets.

It's not easy to transport the tropics to London. Standing in front of this table laden with hammocks, sandals, bows and arrows, and the many colourful headdresses among which my great-grandfather's now casually nestles, I begin to understand just how strange the whole endeavour is. While the curator, wearing white gloves, approaches these history-filled cabinets – on whose sides someone had written 'Beware: possibly toxic' – I stand off to one side studying the beautiful leather labels on which are catalogued the history of various cultures that seem to me, on this London afternoon, terribly remote. I have only to glance out the window of the gallery to realise that we are far from the torrid zone. This gloomy, sterile space is leagues from the muggy mosquito-filled savannah where Schomburgk found these artefacts.

Even so, if you focus, if you allow yourself to be transported, if you carefully play the game, then there are moments when, with that same incredulous wonder the German explorer must have felt, you forget the cold and believe you see the dreamed-of tropics. It is then that you understand why, after the success of the industrial revolution, the British devoted themselves to creating gardens. Hothouses, terrariums, Wardian cases and conservatories: temperate microcosms in which tropical fauna could feel at ease and in which it was possible to cultivate the illusion of eternal spring.

This Victorian spring would be incomplete without *Victoria regia*. It was my grandfather who passed on this piece of history. How, having witnessed the failure of early attempts to bring these water lilies to the metropolis, the botanists of Empire took the reins. William Hooker, Regius Professor of Botany at Glasgow University, the recently appointed inaugural director of Kew Gardens, was determined that the Royal Gardens could not be without the Queen's flower. Together with Joseph Paxton, who was responsible for the gardens at

Chatsworth House, seat of the Duke of Devonshire, Hooker masterminded efforts to recreate a biosphere in which the plant could be cultivated.

While Sororeng was losing himself in the streets of Soho, with its brothels and its gin palaces, Hooker was arranging for seeds to be shipped back to the capital. While Schomburgk's *Indian family* were visiting the Gardens of the Zoological Society of London and the shops of Regent Street, Paxton was busy creating a perfect hothouse, one that would be able to house the daydreams of Sir Walter Raleigh. After various failed attempts, plants that died and seeds that refused to germinate, the first flower budded in Chatsworth on a Wednesday in 1849, floating on the surface of one of the pools Paxton had constructed inside the Great Stove, the largest glasshouse every built.

By this time, Schomburgk was already far away. He had accepted a post as British Consul to the Dominican Republic. Late in life, he retraced the steps of Columbus, never imagining that the flower that had marked the beginnings of his career was now growing within the boundaries of the metropolis. Transporting the tropics was a matter of learning to dream in the depths of winter, just as passers-by had perhaps imagined they were dreaming when, nine years earlier, they saw Sororeng, Saramang and Corrienau wandering the streets of Piccadilly. They could not know that, while their fellow countrymen were tilling gardens, the Guyanese jungle had already begun its long pilgrimage towards ruin.

A simple tale of revenge, Isabel said; she says it again now, as though to underline the fact that all dreamers must someday awake. And the story of Sororeng slowly unfurled like a cruel counterpart to the odyssey of the flowers whose names I had memorised as a boy. Taking from the shelf a timeworn copy of *Travels in British Guiana, 1840-1844,* by Richard Schomburgk, the curator points to a paragraph which mentions an incident that occurred that same spring, after the failure of The Guiana Exhibition.

One afternoon, while visiting the apartment on Golden Square, Schomburgk's brother found Sororeng sitting silently in a chair, looking distressed. Asking what the matter was, he heard this story which now, in mid-afternoon, seemed to echo around the British Museum. He heard how that same afternoon Sororeng had heard that his only living relative, the sister for whom he had been collecting all manner of coins and necklaces, had been murdered by shamans of the Kanaimà. Richard Schomburgk assumed that all this was merely the product of some nightmare, that cold and loneliness had finally seeped into the poor man's dreams. An anguished Sororeng corrected him. This was not a dream, it was a devastating, implacable certainty, one that had come to him that afternoon. The Kanaimà had killed her, and he was to blame; it was his punishment for leaving to work for a white man.

The word *kanaimà* must have sounded strange to the ear of Richard Schomburgk, just as it did to mine when Isabel first uttered it. When he first arrived in Guyana, his brother Robert had heard of the Kanaimà's powers, and indeed began to fear that his expedition was in danger from this evil spirit that was said to attack adventurers at midnight, with an invisible poisoned arrow. Being respectful of the jungle, Robert Schomburgk had the natives in his group create an effigy of a white man, which was placed in a canoe and sent downriver as a sacrifice to the spirit.

To him, Kanaimà was an invisible, omnipresent spirit that cloaked the jungle in death. He had felt its presence, heard its silent footfalls in the darkness. But to his brother Richard, who had not yet travelled to the tropics, it could not be anything more than a superstition. And so, that afternoon, he listened to Sororeng's lamentations with the paternalistic attitude of one listening to a man mired in superstition and magic. Years later, when he finally dared to cross the Atlantic with his brother, he instantly realised his mistake. This was much more than mere superstition, indeed more than simply an evil spirit: Kanaimà was the response of the jungle to the violence that encircled it.

As they struggled to survive in the savannahs and the mountains teeming with missionaries, slavers and rubber plantation workers, the local tribespeople found themselves trapped in a brutal hall of mirrors. Now, even death did not belong to them. Kanaimà was an attempt to reappropriate death in a world increasingly filled with pistols and gunpowder. A world of national borders that had little to do with the jungle as they knew it. Sororeng had fallen into the clutches of this wave of violence which had already seen the Parvilhana population reduced to a handful and which, with the death of his sister, now threatened to deliver the death blow.

That afternoon in Soho, Sororeng did not feel the need to explain any of this. He said only that all this was just a simple tale of revenge: he had gone to work for the white man and the death of his sister was the consequence of his actions. Perhaps, in the waning afternoon, he looked at the necklaces and the coins he had collected for her and realised that, when he returned home, there would be no one left to give them to.

I imagine Sororeng sitting in his room, believing himself to be a man with an inheritance, but no heirs. And I think of the long slipstream left by stories when they come to their supposed end, the invisible trace that lingers and that, one day, prompts us to retrace steps and explore genealogies. I don't know who gave Sororeng's headdress to the missionary who later sold it to my great-grandfather, I can only imagine the threads that connect my world to his.

On those afternoons when he used to show me his paintings, my grandfather liked to tell the tale of how these huge waterlilies inspired The Great Exhibition of the Works of Industry of All Nations of 1851. Paxton, the gardener at Chatsworth, based the edifice on his Great Stove, the conservatory in which *Victoria regia* had first flowered. This glasshouse in which a dream had blossomed seemed the perfect place to encompass a whole world. Neither Schomburgk nor Sororeng were among the multitude who, in the spring of 1851, flocked to Hyde Park to see the formidable edifice of glass and cast iron whose inventors had appropriately named the Crystal Palace.

One person who was there on that May morning was Queen Victoria who, having strolled through the principal galleries, was walking past a statue that caught her eye: an imposing bronze sculpture of an Amazon warrior on horseback. 'Magnificent,' the young queen is said to have written in her diary that evening, though she could not possibly imagine that the word immediately conjured the lands of the Kanaimà where this story had begun, and where Sororeng, lost among alien tribes, now told stories of the elephants and the giraffes he claimed to have seen in the Zoological Gardens in London.

Facial expressions and representations guided Lina Meruane's exploration of the Latin American mask collection, which brings together more than 700 hand-made depictions of humans and animals. Her interest in organs and the role of bodies at an anthropological and philosophical level unfolds in several of her works. She chose to work with four masks with prominent lips and tongues. According to the Bolivian National Museum of Ethnography and Folklore, the trait of the tongue sticking out, present in all four masks, portrays fatigue due to slave labour. These masks belong to Bolivian dances called 'negrerías' and 'morenadas' and are associated with specific characters from the dance: the moreno (pictured), rey moreno, caporal, and probably jukumari. Indigenous, Afro-descendant, and Catholic traditions framing the birth of Jesus converge in these folkloric displays from the Altiplano. The writer discovers in the idea of the mask and its specificity the potential for a metaphor that can develop a layered reflection on the expression of the face.

Recently, these folkloric dances have been strongly criticised in Latin America because of their colonial legacy and stereotypical imagery which promote discriminatory discourses towards Indigenous and Afro-descendant communities. Within this context, Meruane's selection coincided with another SDCELAR project, in which the Afro-Bolivian artist Sharon Pérez offers a critical interpretation based on the Andean dance collection at the British Museum, reflecting on the politics of representation. The writer's challenge consisted of harmonising this subject with the purpose of her story, without appropriating a discourse that does not belong to her as she is not an Afro-descendant. In a fascinating literary game, the author unfolds several levels of analysis surrounding this facial expression. The writer brings the issue of Afro-representation into a domain where the 'tongue sticking out' is simultaneously an image of and protest against the hegemonic system that rules the so-called Western world.

Magdalena Araus Sieber

TONGUES HANGING OUT

Lina Meruane

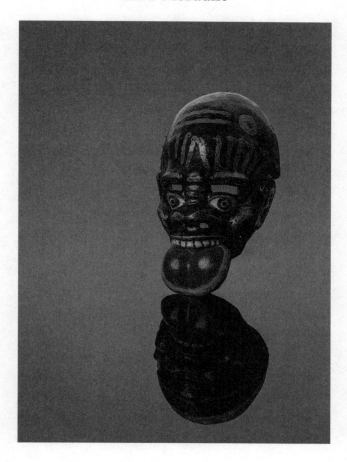

TONGUES HANGING OUT

Lina Meruane

Translated by Megan McDowell

> *The tongue truly expresses a deep malaise.*
> Julio Ramos

with our tongues hanging out:

That's how we get through life, just like that, working too much, you, me, all of us, by working extra hours: that's how we go on living, our mouths open, tongues peeking out as a sign of our exhaustion. Because those of us who don't have one overdemanding job have two or three: part- or full-time jobs, simultaneous and badly paid or paid below their worth. Jobs that consume and sometimes kill us.

In the long pandemic months we've suffered through, not only did we not stop working (those who didn't lose our jobs), we didn't do anything else; locked inside our houses, we worked more than ever.

We thought that would keep us sane amid the most absolute uncertainty.

That uncertainty, perhaps paradoxically, showed us something that was far removed from sanity: in our houses, the productive logic that ruled us outside them had only intensified, and if in the past our exhaustion had kept us from thinking about (feeling, suffering over) what we were doing with our meagre lives, the fear of an unexpected but imminent death forced us to confront the question.

(To think about our lives outside of work — that strange luxury.)

While some of us had to speed up in this crisis to meet even more demanding and ignominious goals than before, others came to a full stop. They gave themselves the luxury of thinking about what they wanted for the time they had left of life. They saw that it did not make sense to work constantly.

Some said goodbye to the abusive boss, licking their lips, opening their mouths, sticking out their tongues for once, for that last time. Someone talked about the joy of slamming the door on your way out, as if the door were a stiff tongue now returning to its mouth and closing it.

extra hours:
Maybe it was during those days, while I was reading the news about massive resignations in my city and across the whole country; while I noted that the extraordinary abdication of four and a half million people in the United States in a single month was being referred to as 'the Great Resignation'; while I also learned that in China the 9-to-9 workdays six days a week was provoking the collapse of white- and blue-collar workers, that there had been deaths by spontaneous combustion and anxiety-induced suicides; perhaps that was when I started to

wonder if what they all felt was something more than frustration, permanent fatigue, headaches and joint pain, stomach cramps and loss of appetite, the insufficiency or impossibility of sleep – I wondered if they weren't more like modern-day slaves. Slaves to something they thought they had chosen and for which they had even competed with others. The horror of exploitation never ended, but merely changed shape. Now it was self-exploitation, but it wasn't voluntary, not exactly. Because behind it was job insecurity and economic inequality and the need to survive without help of any kind – that was the economic strategy employed by some to force others into ceaseless work. Consumed by the competitive logic of every man for himself, we had not only acquiesced, but also agreed to add hours to our work days. As if we were flaunting a power, as if we possessed a superior virtue.

(Tell me how much you work and I'll tell you who you are – that slavery.)

the unsayable:
At what point had I abandoned my unhurried way of life to subject myself to the incessant turning of the wheel?, I wondered. And, thinking of the need – monetary, but also psychological – to prove that one is too busy for any distraction, I likewise came to recognise the anguish brought on by the very idea of working less, or by the idea of quitting, like the millions of others who had left their jobs.

extractivism:
In the extreme extractivism of slavery, the inescapable exploitation of slaves and their children, who inherited disadvantage from their progenitors, I found a key: slaves had been the original cogs in the capitalist system, and if they were eventually freed, it wasn't because of the

humanitarian beliefs of an intellectual elite. Rather, it was because the industrial elite realised that the market, if it was to be viable and grow, would require ever more consumers. If the slaves took jobs, if they received remuneration, if they became responsible for their needs, they would become voluntary slaves of money.

a face that is not the same:
Their bodies – look for their bodies and especially their faces: three curators from the British Museum invited me to the archives to find some object that called out to me, and I thought I would look for the enslaved bodies, their faces. And I thought that finding and identifying them would be possible, because a face is never identical to another face, a face is always unique, and unique are each of its parts. It's an identity that is at the same time multiple because it is the product of accumulation, of the sedimentation of strata. But there was almost no record of the enslaved faces, and then I understood that only *individuals* possess a face and a proper name: working bodies are always one single body, an undifferentiated body that, once exhausted and deemed terminal, is declared expendable. The faces of work have met the same fate.

peer:
Those faces did not exist in the archive but they lived behind our own, as if our faces were their masks and they were simply hiding behind them, peering out through the holes of our eyes.

masquerade:
In the British Museum's archive I found ceremonial masks created in the Americas over centuries of European domination and the centuries that came after:

all of them permeated with the logic of colonial extractivism. For some time, it was believed that they were
celebratory masks that conferred supernatural powers on
the people who wore them, as well as an authority they
didn't have in real life. But later those masks had become
more of a mediation for the mockery the slaves suffered.
My fingers paused on those metal masks rescued from
Bolivian *negrería* dances. They were only a century old,
and referred back to the black people who had served
in the army (and *served* was a manner of saying that they
had given their hides for a nation that would erase them
from its history). These masks called up their memory,
the Tundiqui drums or the onomatopoeic Tuntuna,
tun-tun-tun. They were sad and beautiful, those masks that
were blackened but carefully touched up in gold, with
blue eyes, round and deep, long blond eyelashes, a red ball
on the tip of the nose. One of the masks, the leader of
the *moreno* troop, wore a crown; another, the overseer that
guarded them, had black locks hanging from the back of
its neck; another one held a big wooden pipe between its
lips, defying gravity. But all of them had an enormous red
tongue sticking out from their mouths.

Mouths that my mouth wanted to imitate.

slip of the tongue:
I wrote back to the Museum's curators asking them to
explain the thick, racialised lips on the masks and those
fat tongues, about the conjectures of the specialists that
had oozed like saliva all around them. One or all of them
wrote back saying that little was known for certain,
because flesh and blood black people – *morenos* – did
not have the right to history or to records, and that the
morenada dance was the evidence that they had existed,
that they had eventually been freed from exploitation in
the silver mines, but that those masks were also a form of

stereotyping and mocking the African slave trade in the Colony. Some specialists thought that the dances could have arisen in the Christian *autos sacramentales* (a form of religious play originating in Spain), which dramatised the fight between Christians and Moors, or that their origins might even be traced back to the pre-Hispanic world. And when I consulted the curators as to whether the use of the masks could have arisen then, some said no, that at least those, the ones of the *negrería* dances, came later, because Afro-descendants were not native. And they added that the '*bailes de los negritos*' were criticised today by Afro-descendants, because the dances had been used to ridicule them. And for all the meticulous historical and religious notes I took, what was left stuck to my pale, exhausted lips were these last impressions, the words *ridicule* and *parody* sticking to those mocking masks.

dirty-mouthed silence:
By sticking out their tongues, children avoid talking back. The gesture says it all, and in that dirty-mouthed silence they elude the order of the well-spoken and well-disciplined word in the mouth, the choreography of the face, imposed by *civilisation*. Sticking out the tongue, then, is to remove oneself from the rules and to mock them; it is refusing to enter the kingdom of the human, defined by its exclusion of the animal kingdom's language. Using the tongue to distance oneself from the guttural, on the other hand, means entering the serious world of work. Sticking out the tongue is not, then, an inconsequential gesture, but rather a declaration of absolute resistance to the rules.

play on words:
Those masks sticking out their tongues – are they dirty-mouthed or clean?

lingual verbs:

Sacarla. Mostrarla. Enseñarla. Stick it out. Show it. Teach it. They don't seem to be referring to the same tasks, those verbs. So I read, in these days of research, in an insightful essay where the critic Julio Ramos explained that *enseñar* – to show, but also to teach – a tongue was the pedagogical action of introducing the rules of a language to illiterate people. He added that the other verb, *mostrar* (to show), alluded to the diagnostic scene in which the patient assumes 'the risk of placing their body under the scrutiny of the medical gaze, turning the tongue, metonymically, into the place where the doctor reads the symptoms of illness suffered by the entire body.' The tongue was, in the moment of reading, not a blank page, but rather a slimy and foul-smelling surface where the specialist has access to the enigmatic message that the examined body's owner could not decipher for him or herself. It becomes clear that the black masks of the museum neither *enseñaban* nor *mostraban* their tongues, so it must be that they stuck them out, *las sacaban*. But the linguist believed that if they were stuck out it was because they *didn't have* anything to say or because they *didn't want* to say anything. I had to disagree, because even if they didn't want or were unable to, they had to be expressing something: as Paul Watzlawick has said, it is impossible not to communicate, and all communication carries content.

long in the tooth:

Those protuberant tongues in the faces of the slave become Moor, become soldier, become tireless modern-day worker, went on questioning me during the nights of insomnia under a cloud of pending tasks. What were they warning me about? What were they saying? What was hidden behind those tongues that were put on display with such aplomb? And why were there so many of those tongued masks conserved in that British archive? Because, with my eyes irritated from lack of sleep, the computer in bed and my fingers on the keys, new search words at the ready, I found that those plaster tongues proliferated in the Museum in other masks belonging to all shades of men, that they peered out from the masks of fabulous animals and demonic figures with long, colourful ears: their tongues long in the tooth.

speaking in tongues:
The tongue hanging out is a wagging tongue and a sharp tongue and 'to speak in tongues' happens when one is possessed by the devil.

tongue twister:
Christians must have got the idea somewhere that the tongue, more than other body parts, was sinful. Much as the first church fathers insisted that the tongue in and of itself was not evil, much as Saint Augustine established that only a dirty mind could dirty the distant tongue, that evil tongues are the ones that slander and slur – even so, it was already instilled in the medieval mind that the tongue was an attribute of the devil. Not for nothing does the snake, long, damp, and phallic, have the shape of a tongue. Not for nothing does it seduce with its viperous words. Not for nothing does the devil have a raised tail. And the flames of hell are tongues of fire.

still tongues:
In medieval demonology, the devil and his minions – the sinners who follow him – always appeared with their mouths open and tongues hanging out, while Christ, the apostles and saints who came later, kept their mouths shut even when they were talking. And there was always

the Christian hermit who cut off his tongue to keep from sinning, or the saint who spit hers out to blind her pagan judges, or the other, already tongueless saint who preached the word of God without moving his lips. The divine truth didn't seem to require a fleshly organ to express it, and believers said that the self-same Holy Spirit descended over the apostles like a host of benevolent tongues, spiritual tongues that fought against evil.

exhausted tongue:
I bit my lips, thinking I had gone off course and nearly lost my train of thought. But I kept on reading an essay by Aleksandr Makhov that went back in time to clarify for me that the tongue hanging out precedes Christian iconography by centuries: monstrous Medusa, her hair and tongue on end, was placed outside Greek houses to ward off evil long before the gothic gargoyle decorated the cathedrals, spitting out the rain that eroded facades and frightening off the sinners who eroded the faith. Then I conjectured that those black and white masks represented the feared devil of exploitation who was wearing out their wearers' bodies, and perhaps our own bodies, too. And I thought how we have to open our mouths wide, stick them out, our shiny, pink tongues, our insolent tongues, to beat back the excess work with a curse.

T*his story by Reyes, which tells the origin story of a ceramic head, describes the search by a family of women and girls for an earth goddess who can revive their dry, devastated ecosystem. This fragmented head is part of an archaeological collection bought by the museum in the 1920s, documented as having been made between 500 BCE-500 CE in Manta, Manabí, in coastal Ecuador. During an initial review of the literature on the cultures of the region from this time period, I came across an article[1] written on the* enchaquirados, *groups of men that in ethnohistorical documents are described as harems of religious homosexual servants from the Ecuadorean Pacific coast, not far from the area where the collection was excavated. This article by queer anthropologist O. Hugo Benavides questions early Spanish heteronormative accounts of these groups, as well as their legacy for contemporary Ecuadorean masculinity. Reyes and I agreed that this necessary politicisation of archaeology, which interrogates constructions of gender and sex, made an interesting starting point for framing the collection. Her story draws on Benavides, in the sense of allowing ancient, de-contextualised material culture to describe her version of womanhood. She does not name the women she describes, nor their culture, nor the land they inhabit; even their word for tree is whispered between the narrator and her grandmother – an ancestral knowledge not shared with the reader. However, the story emphasises physicality and tactility – it opens with intimate descriptions of the grandmother's slow, aging movements and ends with moulding lifeforms from clay. Reyes communicates the incarnate experience of imagining an object removed in space, time, and knowledge from its maker.*

Laura Osorio Sunnucks

---

1   Benavides, O. Hugo. 2002. 'The Representation of Guayaquil's Sexual Past: Historicizing the Enchaquirados'. *Journal of Latin American Anthropology* 7 (1): pp. 68–103.

THE NAMES OF THE TREES

Dolores Reyes

THE NAMES OF THE TREES

Dolores Reyes

Translated by Frances Riddle

Big Grandma wakes me up when I nod off. I know there's no time to waste tonight, but exhaustion gets the better of me. I hear Big Grandma call my name again and I stand up from the pile of leaves where I sat dozing. I rush to her and when I get close, I see her clenching her fists, opening and closing them several times. Then Big Grandma moves her feet in little circles and massages her ankles. I can see the pain in her face. Her tired body aches but she forces it to hold on a little longer. There's something important she must do before leaving us for good; she can't die yet. I look at her legs. Years ago I said the word *tree* for the first time sitting on those legs. I was a little girl and she was already the oldest woman on our lands.

'Tree? Which tree?' Big Grandma asked.

And I pointed to the trees around us and said their names one by one.

I look at her legs now, all these years later, violet veins crisscross them like snakes uncoiling across her skin. It feels like a lifetime has passed since I sat in her lap to whisper the names of the trees in her ear. Many of those trees have died, others are very sick. Big Grandma called the six of us girls together to go searching for the goddess of the ground and bring her here so that the trees will stop dying.

I move as close as I can to Big Grandma, cup my hands around my mouth and say *tree* into her ear, like a secret between the two of us. She smiles, forgetting about the pain in her body and for a moment she looks as much like a girl as the rest of us. Big Grandma wants to keep talking. She tells me that when I was very little, I knew the name of each tree without anyone having taught me, that the trees are dying and nothing can protect them. She says once again that we have to find the goddess of the ground so that no more of them will die. She takes both of my hands in hers and looks me in the eye.

'We can't be any more naked than we are without our trees,' Big Grandma says and I don't answer, I just think. The six of us are still just girls and we've never seen the goddess of the ground. We agreed to join Big Grandma, but how will we ever find her? It has to be done at night, because trees are always born in daytime. A seed needs the sun just as a shoot, a stem, a branch, and each leaf does.

'We're going to return their names to the ground so that tomorrow, the rays of sunlight will transform them back into trees. And if we can't find the goddess of the ground, we'll make our own goddess out of the ground using our bare hands,' says Big Grandma, looking at me as a reminder that it's my job to whisper all the names to the goddess so she can bring them back.

But we've been searching for ages in the darkness and

we haven't found her. We need to reach ground that is not sick from fear nor fire. The seven of us trudge slowly along through the blackness, our bodies bumping into each other.

Will this night never end?

We rest for another while before Big Grandma suggests we set out again. Twelve small feet marching behind her for hours on end through a forest of sick trees. Big Grandma says that these trees must have seen terrible things and we follow her in silence, our heads down, too frightened to touch the scarred trunks. What could a tree have seen to make it sick like that?

We reach the end of the diseased trees and arrive to the edge of a cleared forest. We hesitate for a moment then step onto the charred ground. Each tree is a twisted skeleton, black bones jutting up out of carbonised grasses. We walk in silence. None of us dare to mention the creatures, to even think about them. The creatures who didn't manage to escape, who were burned alive inside the trunks of the trees that until just moments before had been their homes. We advance very slowly, the heat from the fires has subsided and the ashy ground is cold as a corpse beneath our feet. I think of Big Grandma and her body that will soon die. I know it's only for us that she's trying so hard to find the goddess of the ground. Then she's going to leave. I hope I never have to see Big Grandma's lifeless body. A few yards ahead, a tree calls to me in a weak voice. Its roots have not yet fully dried up and it's still alive, barely. I move closer without saying anything to the others, who watch silently. The tree whispers its name, which slips into my body. I cover my mouth with my hands to keep from saying it aloud. I stand for a moment before the tree as it dies, its name trapped in my mouth. Big Grandma hugs me. I'm not ready to set the name free. The dying tree is not yet gone as long as its name still remains inside me. This name represents all the dead trees of the world. I don't want to let it go but Big Grandma tells me to say it, that it's time to invoke the goddess. Big Grandma sings to the goddess for hours as we sit around her. Her voice guides the tree into death, but no goddess appears. We wait patiently, but the goddess of the ground does not come. Ancient tears slide over Big Grandma's wrinkled face as she says again:

'We have to return the names of the trees to the ground so that new ones may be born.'

When Big Grandma stops speaking, six girls and an elderly woman set out once again, retracing the steps of a lost goddess.

Will this night never end?

The eldest sister voices the question and we look at each other without daring to speak. Only Big Grandma answers. She says that this night will be long and that it may be the most important night of our lives, but that yes, eventually, like everything, it will end.

I can't stop looking at her. I don't want to think about Big Grandma's life ending, that body I love so much turning to dry bones to be consumed by the sad ground. I take off running. The eldest rushes after me. I run for the riverbank. She is only a couple of years older than me but that is enough of a difference and she easily catches up. Instead of trapping me, the eldest runs past and gets to the riverbank before I do. The other four are much younger than us and couldn't keep up, but the living trees near the water's edge whisper that the girls are not far behind. We laugh and catch our breath listening to the river lap against the dark land. We are glad to hear the sounds of water and to see on its surface the reflection of the moon, whose light shines down onto three canoes.

We stand looking at the canoes and I know that the eldest and I have the same idea: if we take a canoe and go out on our own we could search for the goddess more quickly, before first light.

'But we can't,' says the eldest, dashing my hopes. 'Everything we do tonight must be the seven of us together. If Big Grandma says it's okay, then we can all go out to search on the water.'

I don't answer, I just think. Why would the goddess of the ground wander over the waters?

The other four girls arrive, the last one to get there is the youngest, Big Grandma hanging onto her small arm. To our surprise, Big Grandma isn't mad at us for running off and when we point out the boats and explain our idea, she agrees. We climb into the canoes and push off, gliding over the water. Big Grandma finds a bowl in our canoe and fills it. No one feels sleepy any more, the youngest dips her feet into the dark current. We are guided by the stars of deep night, the moon, and the silence that presses in on us. We continue searching for the goddess; she is present in all places but doesn't want to show herself in any of them. The wind rejects us, forbidding the canoes from venturing downriver.

'What are we going to do?' the youngest asks and right away Big Grandma tells her not to lose hope, that the search is like a game. I watch them talking as the wind pushes us into a bed of reeds, tries to force us back to shore. In our boat only I row, Big Grandma cradles the bowl of water as if it were a treasure, and the youngest stares into the river. The shore is now void of all trees. Everything is darkness and silence. I count my movements mechanically; I make over two hundred paddle strokes but the current is still trying to push us to land. The canoe with the eldest and another sister follows right behind ours and the third canoe is further back.

The youngest changes position, now trailing her hair in the water instead of her feet. She hangs upside down for a while like a ripe fruit, until she gains enough confidence to dunk her entire head under the surface.

'I see something beautiful in the middle of the river,' she says, sitting back up in the canoe. She has completely soaked her thin waist and her budding breasts. I observe the youngest through new eyes. We need to see the goddess's face so that we may recreate it from mud and something tells me that she will look a lot like our littlest sister, who refused to stay in bed, safe at home, when she found out we were going in search of the goddess. I set down the paddles. The canoe doesn't drift but remains in place, rocked gently by the current. I ask the youngest what she saw and in response she kneels in the bottom of the boat, leans over the edge, and submerges half her body.

I crouch beside her, grip the edge of the canoe, and copy her movements. My eyes take a moment to adjust but soon I can see. Water creatures, undaunted by our intrusion, swim up to us, their bodies glimmering with impossible, hypnotic colours.

The face of the goddess appears to us in the water creatures. She has a mischievous grin and her eyes seem to smile.

We surface, too breathless with excitement to speak. Balancing in the canoe, the youngest looks at the water as the rest of us observe her reflection on the surface, replaced by the image of a smiling woman, opening her arms to us. She looks so much like the youngest that they could be mother and daughter. We are euphoric.

The youngest's reflection aligns perfectly with the face of the underwater goddess, then the image of the woman disperses. Immediately we plunge our heads into the river to get another look at the goddess of smiling eyes. Only Big Grandma remains seated upright in the canoe. She says she doesn't need to see, she trusts in us.

Multiple goddesses with smiling eyes and scaled bodies glitter beneath the surface for the six of us to see. We're almost out of breath but we memorise the face of the goddess before the phosphorescent fish disperse. Our bodies are slippery and we are happy as we pick up the paddles. The three canoes begin rowing back to land. We move in silence, glad to have met the goddess, but solemn: a great task still remains. We must now reconstruct that beautiful face and smiling eyes with our bare hands.

Will this night never end?

Using the sheer strength of our arms, we row back to land. We walk away from the riverbank and past the shelter of the trees until we are among new grasses that have not been razed by fire or by the fear that the flames leave in their wake. We form a circle in the clearing. Above, the moon is a red eye staring down on our endless night. We need the trees. We are exhausted but our mission gives us strength. We sit down, our legs splayed, and begin grabbing at the ground, working it with our hands as if they were shovels. We break up the surface of the land, befriending it until it softens and gives up fresher soil. We make cups of our hands but the dry dirt crumbles and slips through our fingers. Big Grandma brings the bowl of water from our canoe and pours a bit onto each of our palms. She once again invokes the goddess in unknown tongues. She cries as we mix our piles of churned up earth together so that it belongs to us all. Twelve hands work in concert as Big Grandma sprinkles water and tears onto them. Then she empties the rest of the liquid onto the dirt. The wet earth no longer tries to escape our fingers. Big Grandma passes the bowl around so we can place our mud inside and take turns kneading it. Then the youngest begins to shape it. We try to help her at first but then let her take over. The rest of us stand and stretch. We begin to dig, using the bowl that is now empty as well as sticks and branches. We dig for hours like wild dogs, clawing at the dirt with our nails. We dig a pit so large we can all fit inside it. We pull at the earth with our flesh, with our nails, with our mouths, and when the hole is deep enough, the youngest comes over. In her outstretched palms she holds the goddess of the ground, looking up at us mischievously out of two black eyes. She seems to smile when the youngest calls her Sister and the rest of us repeat her name. We bake her in the womb of the earth. The ground smoulders and smoke rises from the chimney of mud that Big Grandma instructed us to leave open.

We repeat Big Grandma's prayers without knowing what they're saying. We recite them for hours, under the red moon, loud enough for Sister to hear us underground. We wait until the fire has consumed all of the branches and leaves. Only the stones that we placed on top of the mound remain intact. We let the worst of the heat escape, then we break open the ground little by little, spreading the dirt with branches. We pull our Sister from the naked earth. Fourteen eager eyes look down at the face of the goddess. Big Grandma cackles with glee. She is satisfied and so the six of us allow ourselves to be pleased as well.

The youngest is mesmerised, she stares unblinking at the face of the goddess and finally speaks: 'I am,' she says, then quickly covers her mouth so no more words can escape.

Instead of reprimanding her, Big Grandma stretches out an arm and pulls her small body close: 'Yes, you are the goddess, too,' she says.

The youngest, the littlest of us all, imitates the expression of our goddess and we all smile.

'The trees will come back to life,' Big Grandma says, then she lies down near the open pit.

She tells us that she doesn't want to walk any more or to go back with us, that she's going to stay right here and we have to leave her. Her old body is racked with pain and she curls into a ball as if remembering that she, too, was once a girl. Her body rests. We stand around her without knowing what to do. Big Grandma tells us once again that we should go back without her and for the first time she looks small, much smaller than any of us. I see her shrunken body beside the hole that served as an oven and I want to cry, but I can't. My love for her is a stinging pain deep inside me. We let her rest a while then beg her to stand, but Big Grandma won't change her mind. She's not going to budge from that spot and we all know it. Without saying a word, we place our twelve footprints beside each other in the mud, leaving our mark on the land so that Big Grandma can see it and remember us until the end. It will take many days but her body will serve as food for the seeds, for the small sprouts that will grow into trees, into homes for other creatures, into protection, shade, and shelter. I say the names of the trees that no longer exist, even though I don't know who named them, one by one, like babies as they were born. The names fall to the ground as seeds beside Big Grandma's body. She stretches out an arm to push them into the pit. When she stops moving, we leave.

We walk in silence. The youngest and the other littler ones hold onto each other for support, but the eldest and I walk side by side with our backs straight. We take turns carrying Sister in our hands. Big Grandma told us that the goddess we were searching for was a girl just like us, and that she would protect us always from down beneath the ground, from high up in the trees, and sometimes even from below the surface of the water. Where we met her. In the depths of the river in the depths of the night the goddess had a shimmering scaled body and she showed herself to the six of us. A water creature with the face of a mischievous girl.

We return home, after staying awake for the longest night of our lives. Our eyes have now witnessed both birth and death; we will never be girls again.

Exu is an orixá (god) in the Candomblé religion of Brazil. Eshu is an orisha of the Yoruba religion in Nigeria. Despite the different spellings, Exu/Eshu are the same deity, a trickster who is often regarded as the bridge between humanity and the other orixás. As a counterpart to Ifa, the god of divination, Exu considers that the past can be modified through choices made in the present. Djamila Ribeiro is interested in precisely these transatlantic links between Latin America and Africa. Ribeiro chose to work with objects in the Africa collection to draw out these connections in all their specificity. Although the documentation of African religious objects in the Latin America collection does not make specific reference to Candomblé, the museum's Africa collections house many items related to the worship of Eshu in Nigeria. Djamila Ribeiro employs the object to discuss the role of Candomblé from a personal perspective, as a convert later in her life, and its wider history in Brazil. Candomblé, as an African religion, has typically been practised in secrecy to avoid persecution. As with many African religions in the Caribbean and Latin America, attempts to repress expression continue to this day and Ribeiro's work challenges the systems which allow that to happen. The staff of Eshu was donated to the museum in 1956 by Margaret Plass and her husband Webster Plass, who were avid African art collectors. They resided on the African continent for many years and donated to many museums. This particular staff of Eshu depicts various characteristics of the traditional representation of the orixá. Kneeling with hands joined, Eshu wears his signature long, curved headdress and cowrie shells mounted on leather. Ribeiro's work with the object highlights the role of spirituality in the context of diasporic religiosity and an assessment of Candomblé in contemporary Brazil.

María Mercedes Martínez Milantchi

THE STRENGTH OF EXU

Djamila Ribeiro

THE STRENGTH OF EXU

Djamila Ribeiro

Translated by Daniel Hahn

O Exu-Yangui
Prince of the universe and
last to be born
Receive these birds and
the pawed animals that
I have brought to satisfy
your ritual voraciousness
Smoke of these cigars
that come from African Bahia
This flute of Pixinguinha
for you to cry
chorinho songs to our ancestors
I hope these offerings will
please your heart and
delight your palate
A happy heart is
a satisfied stomach and

in the contentment of both
is found the best predisposition
for enacting the
laws of retribution
that secure
the cosmic harmony
Invoking these laws
Do I implore you o Exu
to plant in my mouth
your verbal axé
restoring the tongue
that was mine
that was stolen from me
Breathe Exu your breath
in the depths of my throat
down where sprouts the
bud of the voice so the bud will blossom
opening into the flower of
my old speech
restored by your strength
Mount me on the axé of words
pregnant with your dynamic grounding
and I shall ride Orum's
supernatural infinity
I shall travel the distances
of our Aiyê made from
a dangerous uncertain land[1]

Itãs are phrases from time immemorial that refer to the mythical tales of the Yoruba tradition. 'Exu killed a bird yesterday with the stone he threw today' is one of the best known. Which was why I had no doubts

1   do Nascimento, Abdias. 1983. *Axés do Sangue e da Esperança* ['Axés of Blood and Hope']. Rio de Janeiro: Achiamé/RioArte: p. 31.

about choosing the object representing Exu to inspire this text, a part of the British Museum collection. Exu is the first of the orixás, the lord of the pathway who enjoys a good laugh. The Catholic Church did not wish to understand, so they syncretised him with the devil and persecuted whoever spoke his name. But Exu laughs at that definition, too. Exu is not goodness, nor evil, but contradiction, uneasiness, change. Another itã teaches us how Exu transports oil in a sieve without a single drop falling onto the ground. It is he whom we must always greet first, whether to give thanks, to weep, to pray. Exu speaks every language and likes to be revered. Beyond the singing, the dancing and offerings at the crossroads, he features in Afro-Brazilian thought through orality, as well as in theoretical work produced about him.

The Brazilian philosopher Renato Noguera has spoken of Exu as 'the orixá who opens the way for events to occur. In mythology, when he throws a stone over his shoulder and kills the bird the previous day, Exu reinvents the past. He teaches us that things can be re-inaugurated at any moment.' In that sense, Exu destabilises the conventional notion of time, offering new histories and the very rewriting of the past and reinvention of life. As that tradition teaches us, Exu represents movement, he is the lord of exchanges and the orixá of communication.

In a recent interview, the Babalorixá and doctor of social sciences, Rodney William, also provides interesting elements for our thinking about the notion of time: 'one of Exu's symbols is that snail-shell shaped into a spiral, and the Exu who is the owner of that shell, or of what that shell represents, is called Exu Okoto. He represents the unfinished, and a circularity that is our own thought. That thinking is a circular thinking and our whole dynamic happens according to that logic of circularity.

The Xirê,[2] for example, circles anti-clockwise and is thus a returning, we are returning to our immemorial past which means that we are returning to our ancestry that is the place of our strengthening.'[3]

The Babalorixá and doctor of linguistics from the University of São Paulo, Sidnei Barreto Nogueira, explains the importance of the market, Exu's domain, as the heart of the community, as it is there that exchanges are made. 'Exu's stall has two sides,' one of his powerful lines, teaches us life lessons about reciprocity. In the Afro-Brazilian traditions, the market, here also in a metaphorical sense, 'exists so that the flame of exchanging will remain alive. We need to learn exchanging more than buying. Buying benefits one. Exchanging benefits both. Because the market stall has two sides. It should always have two sides,' says Sidnei Nogueira.

It is these meanings laid out above that I would like to take as my starting-point for considering this text. For the black population who were enslaved and made victims of colonialism, it was necessary to transcend those norms through a path of return and re-signification of time. In this sense, the exchange of knowledge among the African diaspora is a place of power and of continuing to kill the bird yesterday with the stone thrown today.

As a dark-skinned black woman born in São Paulo, I do this exercise of looking at the past to talk with the lord of crossroads. I am a black Brazilian woman of the terreiro. That means I am a *candomblecista*, that I live by the ethos of Candomblé, an Afro-Brazilian religion. Generally located in rural areas or peripheral regions,

2   *Xirê* in the Yoruba tradition means *wheel*. In the Candomblé tradition, it is the dance circle in celebration of the orixás.
3   William, Rodney. 2020. 'Apropriação cultural e racismo' ['Cultural Appropriation and Racism'], interview by Victor Hugo Neves de Oliveira. In *Revista Coletiva*, issue 28: p. 4.

'terreiros' are Candomblé communities that, under the leadership of a priestess (Yalorixá) or priest (Babalorixá) recreate the familial, epistemological and religious bonds torn apart by slavery and colonialism.

It is only the strength of my ancestry that has allowed me to reach this year of 2022 and call myself a woman of Candomblé. This is because through the nineteenth, twentieth and twenty-first centuries, Candomblé terreiros were banned, vandalised, set alight. Playing the atabaque used to be a crime, and to this day priests and priestesses find themselves compelled under threat to shut their communities' doors. Where once it was the police, today the neo-Pentecostalists are active, too, as they grow in number just as the Catholic church, while still very powerful, is losing its flock. By neo-Pentecostalists you should understand many variations of Protestant churches, of various sizes, but which have a political identity in common. With the exception of some evangelical church movements that are progressive and minoritarian, one of the precepts that unite them all is an aversion to religions of an African mould. At the root of all this, racism expressed in religious form.

Sidnei Nogueira, the author of an important book in Brazil on the subject, *Religious Intolerance*, quotes in his work a verbalised thought from the Yalorixá Marisa de Oyá, who explains how this intolerance is a reflection of slavery: 'It is a reality that has been established in this country since the end of slavery. What to do with them, if they are no longer slaves? We will eliminate them. It began with the ban on studying, on acquiring lands, on working and living with dignity. Every attempt was made to achieve the extermination of a race. But this people is strong, and resists valiantly, with its faith and the belief in its gods, Orixás, Vodunces, Inkises. And thus Religious Racism is created, in order once again to attack and try to weaken this dark-skinned race, so strong and so beautiful, that neither bends nor loses heart. The violence and vandalism against terreiros is no more than racism and the bright illumination of a people, who were enslaved, and who resist to this day through their ancestries. We shall not fall. We are stronger than anything.'[4]

In the state of Rio de Janeiro, for example, with its strong tradition of terreiros, recent years have seen a multiplying of violations against these communities by 'traffickers of Christ', that is, the 'owners' of communities abandoned by the state, who will not accept a black religion in the areas they control. These traffickers of Christ are one piece of straw in a matted hay-bale of that evangelical identity. It is important to stress that nowadays neo-Pentecostal churches own TV and radio networks, have a presence in every city in Brazil, in addition to a whole bunch of councillors, mayors, governors, deputies, senators, ministers, and even the president to establish their project of power in the country and in other places around the world, including several countries on every continent.

To present this scenario of a Brazil that persecutes the religions of the atabaque, of dancing and black faith, is to refute the image that gets exported of a 'racial paradise', where white, black and indigenous people transcend racial conflicts and live together harmoniously in samba – a musical rhythm, incidentally, that was born in the terreiros, and I must pay tribute here to the great Yalorixá Tia Ciata (1854-1924). Dismantling the imagined picture of racial democracy has been an exercise of Ogum by the Brazilian black community for a long time. black intellectuals like Abdias do Nascimento, Lélia González, Sueli Carneiro, Kabengele Munanga, among many

---

4   Nogueira, Sidnei. 2020. *Intolerância Religiosa* ['Religious Intolerance']. São Paulo: Sueli Carneiro/Editora Jandaíra): pp. 86-87.

others, have produced vast output on the subject. Just as a reminder, this is a country where, every eight minutes, a woman is the victim of rape,[5] the great majority of these black women, and where every 23 minutes a young black man is murdered.[6] Around here, black women receive the lowest salaries and are the main targets of attacks on social media.[7] Laws have prevented black people from studying, like the 1824 Constitution, and made it impossible for them to acquire land, as in the Land Law of 1850. As the last country in the Americas to abolish slavery, it did not adopt any measures to include the recently freed population, but it did naturalise 'destinies' for black people. As for black women, more than 6 million are still in domestic service today. This is the context in which the Candomblé black community has resisted.

Today the backward steps have been many and the victories achieved by the Black movements at the end of the nineties and during Lula and Dilma's progressive mandates are under fierce attack. I am writing this in January, in the year of presidential elections in Brazil. It is the fourth and final year of the mandate of Jair Bolsonaro. But the message I would like to get across here is this: even after centuries of persecution and four years of Bolsonaro, the terreiros remain strong, proud of their axé and ready to assert themselves as political spaces. Bolsonaro finds his own political supporter base in the Christian churches that proliferate in poor communities, stepping into the role of the State. These poor communities have race running through them, woven into a sophisticated web that encourages religious racism.

---

5   Data from the 2021 Public Security Yearbook.
6   U.N. data, 2017.
7   Research by Luiz Valério Trindade, at the University of Southampton, to be published in March 2022 under the title *Discurso de ódio nas redes sociais* ['Hate Speech on Social Media'] (Jandaíra/Selo Sueli Carneiro).

Faced with such powerful enemies, who mobilise historical structures rooted in discrimination to distil a religious hatred, it is necessary to construct networks of strategies, intelligence and reverence so that communities might continue with their prayers, their dancing and their festivals to their beloved orixás.

But whoever has Exu by her side can be sure that the war, however unequal it might be, won't come close to putting an end to a people. The lord of paths and crossroads, messenger of the orixás, Exu owns the road. It is worth remembering that the crossroad has a universal symbolic importance, representing the centre and the place of passage between the worlds of humans and gods. It is the home of Exu, who is tasked precisely with linking the sacred to the profane, being the orixá of the dynamic principle that governs existence. While intolerance has grown, so too has resistance. The three intellectuals I have cited are known across the country for their work. Sidnei Nogueira's *Religious Intolerance*, the eighth title in the Plural Feminisms Collection, under my editorship, was a finalist for Brazil's top literary prize. *Cultural Appropriation* by Rodney William, the seventh title of that collection, has been translated into French and is currently on the reading-list for a Master's programme at the Sorbonne University in France. Despite everything, we continue, with Exu's strength, to kill birds from the day before with the stones we throw today.

The piece that inspired Cristina Rivera Garza's story is a sample of the potato plant that nominally belonged to the natural collection at the British Museum until the British Museum of Natural History (1963) was created, dividing 'natural' from 'anthropological' collections. The sample was collected by the English botanist John Gregory Hawkes outside the city of Sucre, Bolivia, in June 1939. This expedition represented a British effort to explore existing varieties of potatoes in their places of origin, a century and a half after the tuber became essential to the Western diet, favouring European dominance in the world. The experiences of Hawkes are described in the publication Hunting the Wild Potato in the South American Andes, and throughout his career, the botanist would establish himself as one of the world's leading scientists in the study of potato taxonomy and the conservation of genetic resources.

Rivera Garza, guided by the spirit of this project, blurs the limits between disciplines by choosing a 'natural history' piece and reframing it within an alternative cultural and political context. Her interest in the potato and this exploratory journey comes from an ongoing creative project, where she imagines a distant future in which a group of women must survive in adverse conditions. Her story shares this same setting, where the tuber becomes an essential element for women who must learn how to harvest their food and re-write its history. Rivera Garza conceives a narration about women of profound resilience, metaphorically projecting what Hawkes wrote about the potato that grows even '...among the rocks on the edge of the fields.'

Magdalena Araus Sieber

LATE BLIGHT

Cristina Rivera Garza

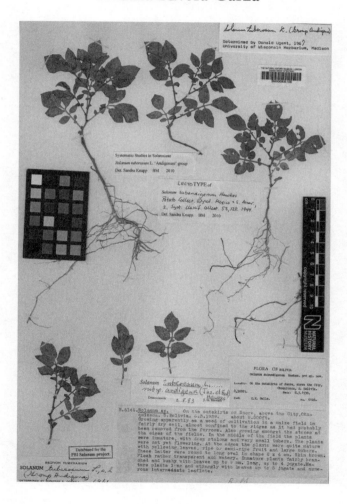

LATE BLIGHT

Cristina Rivera Garza

Translated by Robin Myers

Given everything we know, the Scientists must have been a group of radical relegationist women. It would be hard to believe such a thing if people only heard, and trusted, the version of our origins that Octavania Doñez likes to spread. Come lambs, come deer, come wild boar. Welcome to the flying air. Here we are, stars of immensity. It's true that the Scientists could have left our bodies in some lab, protected by glass walls and precision instruments, but they chose, instead, the farthest corner of a volcano. They could have opted for colonies on Mars or sidereal shuttles, but they abandoned us, instead, on Earth. They believed in the Earth. In the Earth's possibilities.

Which can't help but spark a kind of tenderness.

Retreat from everything: that was their motto. Attain total autonomy in regions of the planet not yet entirely dominated by the interests of capital and the laughingstocks of technique. Their booklets, made of newsprint, stamped with the navy blue ink of a risograph machine, still smell like gunpowder, like rancid food, like the sweat that clings to the body after a violent chase. How to build a house from start to finish. How to level the concrete floor. How to lay bricks into a perfect wall. How to identify and exchange DNA sequences. How to manufacture a washing machine out of a bicycle. How to cook with solar rays. How to use the layers of the soil as a storage system. How to build a sound system that encompasses entire kilometres. How to card wool. How to milk cows. How to edit cells inside the body in real time. How to plant lettuce in order to make a salad later. How to purify water. How to graft. How to recognise edible mushrooms. How to descend a mountainside at top speed. How to shelter from the cold. How to connect computer cables to the energy of the subsoil. How to bandage. How to equip. How to plant potatoes and how to protect them from the late blight. What to do in case of utter solitude.

In case of utter solitude, it's essential to leave evidence.

In case of danger.

Antonio Rivera Peña stopped the vehicle, taking a moment before he opened the door to study his surroundings through the binoculars strung around his neck. He sighed. Sometimes he did that: sigh. In the face of vastness, which opened out unknowable in his path, but especially in the face of the tiniest obstacles of everyday life, he'd let out a great puff of air. How many days of rocky trails, mountains surrounded by squalls, humble settlements flung far from the hand of god, all for nothing? Irritation, a punctual tide, surged forth again and again to puff out his lips. He slid his sunglasses down to perch on the tip of his nose. A half-lit, half-snuffed pipe hovered almost miraculously, a kind of apparition, between his clenched teeth. The days-old stubble. He was exhausted, a bit fed up with the place, which hardly ever changed. He felt like stretching his legs. He suddenly craved the cup of coffee he'd poured into his thermos that morning. The scent, which wafted up from the hot liquid and crept into his nostrils without asking permission, perked him up completely. He could keep going. He realised he actually wanted to keep going. He took the octagonal compass from his jacket pocket and trained it north. Then, with his pack on his back, he headed for the slope and walked up, towards the northeast, making sure to anchor his boots on steady rocks. He needed pressure on his chest, that feeling of breathlessness, of being about to perish, instantly followed by the opposite feeling. Full lungs. He needed to know he was alive. Was he thinking about Linnaeus? He was often thinking about Carl Linnaeus. A hamlet in the south of Switzerland, two centuries back. The expedition to Lapland. The Botanical Gardens in Uppsala. The new way of naming that changed the way of seeing and of searching. Was he thinking about Sophien Kamoun, who successfully sequenced the *Phytophthora infestans* genome in 2009, proving that it was an extraordinarily long form of mould, longer than any oomycete remotely like it? He thought about Sophien Kamoun and about Chad Nusbaum and about Kris Oboden. He quickened his step when the terrain got horizontal and then stopped, for the sheer pleasure of it, to look out at what remained down below. Distance fascinated him: how villages and tree trunks and their branches, rocks and what they stored beneath them, all shrank under its mantle. A mantle, he repeated aloud, as if he'd just made a discovery. Under the mantle of distance, which expanded with his every step, he felt protected. He sighed. Then, keeping his gaze fixed on the peaks of the volcano, he walked away from the settlements, the little parcels of corn, the sprinklers for the milpas where squash and chillies grew intermingled.

Suddenly the fog covered everything. He knew it would be smart to stop, to take a break and wait for a better moment to return to the truck, but he felt his way forward, unable to make out even the tips of his own feet. It wasn't the first time he'd found himself enveloped in the fog's dense veil, but he'd never before felt trapped in it. He kept moving, because a sensation like claustrophobia accelerated his heartbeat and wrested the air from his lungs. The blackout must have been caused by hyperventilation. He stayed on the ground for a while, completely motionless, once he came to. He saw himself from up above: arms spread, one knee flexed to form an equilateral triangle beside the other, perfectly vertical. What was he doing there? Why so zealously chase after those wild species that were clearly doing everything in their power to elude him? How significant, in the grand scheme of things, especially here in the haze, could a small sequence of ribonucleic acid really be? The questions flooded back all at once. A hare stopped to sniff his static fingertips, then carried on its way. The squawking magpies, which began to wheel around some invisible point in the sky, put him on alert. He had to stand. He couldn't fall. He couldn't give up.

In the notepad tucked into the back pocket of his pants, he jotted down the date in Roman numerals and then, below it, a single line: I won't let the fog defeat me.

Soon after, he saw them. He'd sat up with care, checking slowly that he hadn't broken a bone or torn a muscle. He shook his legs and rubbed the back of his neck when he finally made it to his feet. He picked up his pipe, empty now, definitively snuffed, and returned it to its case, which he placed, in turn, inside his backpack.

At last, he decided to take a step. And then another. He collided a couple of times with trunks severed by deafening saws and stumbled into amputated boughs the paths hid, jumbled together on the ground. He was shaken by the scent of injured wood. He always was. He was sure he had to go back, descending the slope, but even though his breathing told him he was still unquestionably making his way up the mountain, he didn't stop. Some moments are like this, he told himself. Some attractions are stronger than yourself. And he resigned himself to his fate. The first plant appeared a little farther along, among the loose rocks underfoot: some thirty centimetres high, dense, with infinite branches and a green he'd only glimpsed in dreams. Some metres on, he saw the second. And then a third. He took photos, touching them with his eyes before his hands. And he followed them like breadcrumbs in a sinister forest. That was how he came upon the caves in the northwest quadrant of the volcano. He went in silently, slowly, fearing the strikes of wild animals or the attacks of ancestral bacteria. He touched the rough walls, then brought his fingers to his nose. He soon confirmed that there was nothing inside and wondered why. When he stepped out of the cave and took the wind's blow to the face, he got his answer. He looked up: the squall shifted comfortably and with colossal strength around the sky. At the same time, it dragged at the clouds and swirled up and down the mountainsides, shuddering the pine boughs and the meadow higher up. He calculated that the temperature had dropped at least ten degrees Celsius since he'd got there. Maybe more. He could easily picture the lightning bolts crashing against the rock, then the arrival of the summer's most violent downpours. Of course no one lived here. Of course the cave was permanently uninhabited. Sealed off from humanity. Except for them. The plants. Except for these long vertical roots that travelled towards the centre of the earth, loaded with tubers four to six centimetres wide, a thin layer of pale skin filled with eyes and this juicy flesh, packed with starch and vitamin C, slightly acidic to the taste. There was nobody here except for them and these walls of igneous rock, which loomed over the stony ground, frankly dour, with the weight of centuries. There was nobody here but the plants, and now him, rubbing his hands together as quickly as he could, blowing his inner air, his own air, onto his fingers, while, doubling back inside himself, he tried to orient himself among the alleyways of the caves: a labyrinth. A web. He sighed because he didn't know how to do anything else, because it was his automatic response, because it had always been easy for him to mistake joy for annoyance.

And he left all that behind when the buzzing in his ears became a squeal and then a moan. He feared losing his balance again, so he gathered the samples he needed and began his descent. Did he save them in this act, or steal them from the mountain, or was it all the same? As soon as he caught sight of the truck in the distance, he pulled the notepad from his back pocket and sketched, sitting inside the vehicle now, the scene he'd witnessed up above. He calculated the coordinates and took them down. He did the same with the altitude measurements. Then he set out to wrap the leaves and stalks and roots of the potatoes in blank sheets of paper, packing them hard and then tying them shut with ixtle twine. He tucked the tubers into his jacket pockets. When everything was ready, he started the engine and spent a couple of hours inching along the dirt road. The gale, which had forced him to grit his teeth and glimpse the summer storms, seemed to have been a figment of his imagination. Night fell abruptly, and he huffed again, as if finding oneself under a perpetually clear sky was the norm on the mountain. Before he turned onto the highway, Antonio Rivera Peña parked the truck in a ditch, lowered the window, and poked his head out. How many millions of years were culminating in this moment and how many more millions would follow it? Who in the infinite past and who, peering out from the incessant future, could be imagining him now, halted at ground level, face craned towards the cosmos, as they inspected the body of the potatoes with trembling hands, only to bite into them, more captive to despair than to curiosity? Whom had they saved before and whom would they save later, these tubers, momentarily separated from their site, which would return to him stronger, genetically improved, resistant to extant or future diseases? He felt infinitesimal, and the sensation, which relieved him of weight and made him gradually indivisible, came as a comfort. He closed his eyes. When he opened them, he found the absolute glimmer of stars in the firmament.

'They're ghosts,' he reminded himself aloud. 'None of them is really there.'

He'd heard stories about the caves before. The farmers he sometimes chatted with when he stopped to eat would confess their troubles with the late blight, and then, as if it were the very same issue, they'd mention the place, the nape of the mountain, they called it, where it was best not to go.

'Oh really, why's that?' he'd asked them lightly, somewhat sceptical, as he paid for a just-grilled ear of corn or a bowl of fava beans.

'Well, because the people who make it up there don't come back,' they responded several times in several ways and with utter confidence.

Preparing materials in the greenhouse, he recalled as many of those stories as he could: people get stuck there, the cold freezes them through, the howling of the wind drives them mad, the hail riddles their skin, the lightning splits their heads in two, the torrents of water drag them through the labyrinths of the caves into the very centre of the earth. And he smiled to himself. Before him were the first wild specimens he'd extracted, safe and sound, from the caves, ready to begin the long cycle of genetic editing. Planters. Soil. Water. The proper temperature. If everything went well, if things went as he'd sketched at the time, he'd be able to return to the mountain settlements in the not-too-distant future with variations resistant to attacks of late blight. He'd do it, and he jotted that down in his notebook: by himself, without alerting the institute or waiting for the patent paperwork to go through, he'd distribute some samples among the neediest farmers, those who'd suffered the greatest losses and had already resigned themselves to migration, promising to work closely with them in the new cycle. But he'd also do something else. And this too he recorded in the broken contour of his handwriting. He'd select the best seeds, and, applying an ancient method of dehydration, alternating between periods of freeze and sun, he'd make sure they were conserved for the future. Once they were dried out, freed of nearly 80% of their original weight, he'd wrap them carefully in brown paper bags and place them side by side in sacks, which he'd then carry on his back up to the nape of the mountain. He'd look for the caves, and, right where he'd found the hardiest plants, he'd dig a hole, and there, no more than three metres deep, he'd deposit the seed. A repository: that's what he'd make. A storehouse or an offering. A letter to the future. If they were ever needed, the potatoes themselves would show them the way. Nevermore those dark stains cropping up on the leaves and stalks of the plants like a genuine curse. Nevermore the fine white dust and its augury of rot, and then the total loss. Nevermore the hunger. The unease.

Nevermore the stench of putrid, decomposing things that, as he'd been told so many times, you could smell from afar and long before.

The farmers had been on tenterhooks forever. They were ensnared in a futile struggle, one they may have lost from the start, or even before it began, against the invisible, elusive organism that infected their yield. Fungicides, which had worked for a cycle or two, soon proved ineffective. They were hopeful at the onset of the new season, digging the furrows and planting the seeds they'd stored from the previous year, thinking they'd left their condemnation behind, only to realise, weeks later, that the rot was on its way. When temperatures began to rise and the hot spell, usually limited to a couple of weeks a year, expanded into three or four, the rot settled in the region and refused to leave.

'*Phytophthora infestans*,' he murmured, as if referring to a person by their full name.

And I swear, all these centuries later, that it was still possible to hear the voice rising up from the fragile, yellowed pages of a creased notebook we found forgotten among the objects of the archive. Here we are, stars of immensity. Come lambs, come deer, come wild boar. Welcome to the flying air. We repeat the phrases out of habit, not without a certain scorn, and lift our faces skyward. And so we stay, together and quiet for a long time, listening to the unsettling sound of a living thing. Of a thing that has survived.

Velia Vidal came to the museum to see a collection of more than three hundred everyday objects from Chocó, Colombia, the region where she was born and continues to live. Among baskets, jewellery, bows and arrows, bowls, and blow-pipes, she found two wooden stirring sticks tagged with the name 'Otilio'. These were bought along the San Juan river by the ethnomusicologists Brian Moser and Donald Tayler, who travelled through Colombia in the early 1960s and made a collection labelled as 'Indigenous' material, even though Chocó is one of the densest Afro-descendant areas in the Americas. The introduction to Moser and Tayler's book about their field collection, The Cocaine Eaters,[1] was never translated into Spanish, so I translated while reading the introduction aloud to Vidal, who sat and listened to their description of her home region, in which Indigenous inhabitants along the San Juan river are presented as fighting for survival in the context of incursions from the globalised world, in particular Afro groups and commerce. This narrative of Indigeneity pervades the Latin American collection, which with very few exceptions, holds no material attributed to Black or Afro-descendant populations outside of Brazil and the Caribbean. Relevantly, Brazil and the Caribbean are the only two parts of the region not to make Afro groups invisible in their early nation-building projects. Vidal returned to Chocó to request meetings with local leaders and councils along the San Juan, soliciting their thoughts about the collection, the way it represents the region, and how it could now be meaningfully activated by Indigenous and Afro-descendant people. Her first reflection considers the name 'Otilio': the only local name we have among the vast group of things known at the museum as the Moser and Tayler collection.

Laura Osorio Sunnucks

1   Brian Moser and Donald Tayler. 1965. *The Cocaine Eaters*. London: Longman's.

OTILIO

Velia Vidal

OTILIO

Velia Vidal

Translated by Annie McDermott

When my uncle Lino decided to teach me to fish, hunt and work with wood – to be a Wounaan, in other words – I stopped spending hours on end watching the river. I found I was good at whittling and carving, so from then on I used to pass the time shaping every stick that came my way. I got a taste for turning planks into canoe paddles with the blade of a machete, and it wasn't long before I'd learnt to make ladles and chopping boards. I no longer sat for hours under the tambo's thatched roof, watching the San Juan flowing by and the things it carried along, but I never stopped wondering where it all came from and where it would end up, that collection of logs, boats and people travelling down a river so wide it sometimes seemed to have no other bank, like the sea far below, which it reaches through seven mouths, or so say those who have sailed all the way there.

By now I've carved plenty of paddles, chopping

boards, washboards, sieve stands, spoons, and pans for finding gold in the river, but it was about a year after I started learning that I carved my first chingo – my first canoe. It looked so beautiful that I wanted to put my name on it. But I didn't know how to write, so I drew the letters the way my uncle told me. I loved making stirrers, which are long spoons with flat ends that people use for mixing sweets like panela and birimbí. They were fun because I could shape the handles to look like snakes, intertwined half-moons or the big river with all its bends. Across the end of each handle, I also drew the letters of my name. Understanding what I was drawing came later, when Justina, my godmother, suggested that my mum send me to the house of some missionaries who discussed religion and taught people to write, at least well enough to sign their initials. No one knew quite how they came to be there, but they'd settled in with such confidence that they seemed like life-long neighbours.

Perhaps to encourage me with my writing, my mum gave me a gold bracelet that she'd been left by my dad. The moment I saw it, I recognised the letters written on the metal and knew we had the same name. That was really exciting. She also told me a fuller version of her life story, which I'd heard bits of during her conversations with my godmother, as they sat drinking viche liquor and joking about what the black people said about the Wounaan and the Wounaan about the black people. They laughed at their luck: Justina hadn't been able to have children and it was like a curse, she said, because her husband Antonio had used it as an excuse to make another home in Palestina. She pretended not to know. Someone had even pointed the kids out to her when she'd been passing that way, on one of her trips to the city to be seen by the doctor who prescribed her a treatment that didn't help at all, any more than the herbal tonics did, or the prayers to Santa Ana, patron saint of fertility, which she was encouraged in by Sister Victoria, one of the missionaries.

My mum was the second wife chosen by Plácido, a Wounaan from here in the community who dreamed of going off to Panama, as did most men at the time. They thought that over on the other side, as they called it, you could find weapons and all sorts of things we didn't have here. They needed the weapons for hunting and for the day when war would break out against the black people, a conflict that had been brewing ever since the blacks first began to be freed and make their way down the river in groups of one or two families to build their houses on the bank, and more and more turned up and they began to form settlements. A few dared to challenge a local chief in order to get themselves a bit of land. Meanwhile, most of the Wounaan simply moved deeper into the jungle, up the streams and along the smaller rivers that flowed into the big one. That's more or less how Noanamá stopped being an indigenous village and became a village of black people, with the Wounaan only coming down to buy or trade things, and sometimes on festival days. Still, the war Plácido was expecting never arrived; indigenous people and black people, despite their mistrust, carried on living in peace.

Among the few black people that Plácido liked were Seño Marta and her husband Armando, for a long time the owners of a big shop that sold food, cooking pots, tools and whatever people from the communities brought down, such as plantains or viche. Since they sometimes gave Plácido things on credit, he was happy to paddle my mum to the village in his chingo one week so she could lend Seño Marta a hand, husking the rice and corn and doing other bits and pieces. Justina, who normally helped, was in the city, trying to fix her womb troubles. Seño Marta's place was also where the chirimía dance was held in Noanamá every Friday. The dance was famous in the region because it was a kind of farewell to the river travellers, who set off bleary-eyed and stinking of viche on the Saturday morning boat from Istmina.

The week Plácido took my mum to the village, a malaria man was visiting, the kind who do blood tests and give out medicine and mosquito nets so that fewer people get sick and die. My mum says he was tall, thin and very clean, as if no mud from the riverbank or jungle had ever touched him. The party that Friday was a special one: a marimba player called Señor Petronio had come down from Tadó. He was well known because not only was he very good at playing, but he also wrote his own songs. My mum had been sent to pour viche for the musicians, and that's what she was doing when my dad walked in; they fell in love the moment they saw each other. She heard quite clearly when Martín, the other malaria man, said to his friend: 'Pretty black girls everywhere and you're checking out a chola. Why go asking for trouble? You know that lot don't like us.' But when someone's in love, they won't be told. The next morning, with the sun beating down on the river, he gave my mum the bracelet before heading to the dock, so she wouldn't forget their night together and so she'd know it hadn't been a lie. He told her the bracelet had been made by the Wizard, one of the most famous jewellers in Quibdó.

Plácido was actually pleased when he found out my mum was pregnant, she says, but once she'd given birth he turned up to see me in a fury, because Emiliana, his other wife, had told him I was a mixed-blood zambo and couldn't be his son. So really, he'd turned up to inform my mum that he was off to Panama because she'd made him a laughing stock, and that she'd better plant some guava trees for her ugly little monkey to swing from.

My uncle Lino built a tambo with a thatched roof where my mum and I could live. Justina, who by then was very good friends with my mum, came at least twice a week to help out. They used to cook together and chat. Anything my mother had to sell, Justina took down to the town: chaquira bead necklaces, a basket, a bit of achiote or a few giant passionfruit. She came back with rice, plantains, panela sugar, and sometimes some money. When I was about a month old, my mum asked Justina to give me a name, since she was my godmother. 'You know what his name is, Floricelda,' she replied. 'It's written on the gold bracelet his dad left you.'

I went out hunting with my uncle five days ago, and yesterday, when I got back, my mum was nowhere to be seen. I realised the plate racks and boards I'd recently finished carving were gone as well, along with my two favourite stirrers: a small one, like a toy, and a big one I'd marked with the blue pen that Sister Victoria gave me. I mark and keep the things that turn out the best, and I don't trade them for anything.

Later on, my mum came back pleased because she'd sold them all to some men from the other side who were going around buying things up. She looked so happy that I couldn't be annoyed, but I got in my chingo and rowed down to the village to see if I could find the men. At Seño Marta's, someone said they'd left for Palestina. I wanted to at least get back the stirrer with my name on it; I'd been saving it for when I went to Quibdó to look for my dad. So I carried on down to Palestina, although the journey was longer, but when I arrived I was told the men had gone on to Baja Calima, and I couldn't travel all the way there.

Today I went back to watching the river, wondering where everything that floats past me ends up. What happens to the travellers who never return, like the artist who told the black women to keep still while he painted them on a canvas, or the very white girls who came right into the tambo and left some gifts that are still under the table, or like the four senators who said things no one understood and promised building works no one had asked for – or like my dad? What happens to the things that are carried away and don't come back? Like my chopping boards, my plate racks, my ladles or the stirrer bearing my name and the name of my father: Otilio.

I*n his piece recounting a recent trip to Iquitos in the Peruvian Amazon, Zárate shows a photograph of a feather headdress to Bora leader Liz Chicaje Churay. This item was donated to the British Museum in 1920 by Emilio Kanthack, who was the British Consul in Para and who also owned the Belén-based rubber exportation company, Emilio Kanthack & Co. As our project with Murui-Muina elders Óscar Román and Alicia Sánchez shows, items collected at the time of the rubber boom in some cases constitute a unique glimpse of cultures severely affected by genocide and the forced displacement of communities from ancestral territories – in a context where plants, animals, and invisible forces, as well as people, have rights. They thereby also embody the experience and memory of decades of violence associated with the rubber-tapping industry in Amazonia. While our project ultimately considered this context in terms of the relevance of objects collected through colonial networks during this period of extractivist damage, Zárate's research goes further, to invoke the tensions between the permanence and ephemerality of humanity. The river and photograph he describes remain tangible, for now, but Lili and the village she was born in, Vistoso, are not. This impermanence, he reminds us, is also the condition of the author and readers of the text. Anthropological collecting, which has traditionally been based on concerns about cultural endangerment and extinction, increasingly faces the irony that it is museums, and even humanity itself, that is under threat.*

Laura Osorio Sunnucks

IN THE LAND OF THE WEEPING TREES

Joseph Zárate

IN THE LAND OF THE WEEPING TREES

Joseph Zárate

Translated by Fionn Petch

> *There's a place I know myself*
> *in this world, nothing less,*
> *one we will never reach.*
> César Vallejo

My mother and I may disagree on a number of issues, but never on this one: we both hate cemeteries. Perhaps that is why, since Mamita Lilí died on a December day like today, we have only once gone to leave flowers on her grave. This year, the fifth without her, will be no different. In Lima, my cousins, aunts and uncles are celebrating another mass that we will not attend. My mother says she prefers to remember her this way, without funerary paraphernalia, as she travels across one of the country's provinces in her work as a tools salesperson. For my part,

I've just arrived in Iquitos, on the banks of the powerful Amazon, where my grandmother spent the first years of her life.

I want to believe that I'm here, a thousand kilometres from home, only for work: to write about the capital of the Peruvian jungle, about its past steeped in wealth and in blood, about the rubber plantations and the extermination of whole peoples and cultures, about the indigenous relics that explorers took from this land more than a century ago and today are exhibited in museums in the First World, about how these artefacts tell stories that most of us don't know, about the memory we lost and perhaps will never recover.

I want to believe that I came here for that.

But the truth is that now, as I enter the neighbourhood of Belén, known as the 'Venice of Peru', with its cabins built on stilts over the water, its raucous market and the sweet aromas of fruit, all I can think of is the face of Mamita Lilí appearing everywhere, under this relentless sun. Of the women grilling ripe plantain over glowing red coals. Of the motor-taxi drivers devouring *juanes*, *tacachos* and turtle stew at long tables. Of the girls selling medicinal plants, aphrodisiac nectars, crushed roots. Of the workers drinking beer and listening to technocumbia on a too-loud radio. Of the kids using machetes to slice up doncella, paiche and other fish of extraordinary forms. In all of them, some of her features can be spotted – her elongated eyes, her jet-black straight hair, her copper skin – and some of mine, too: of her twenty grandchildren, I'm the one who looks most like her. And the only one who decided to return to this piece of jungle, with its half a million inhabitants, to write about her.

Perhaps this too is what this story is about.

Sometimes we write only in order to fulfil a promise.

It was the summer of 1939.

Lilí Tuanama Núñez arrived in Iquitos at the heart of the Loreto region when she was still a baby strapped to her mother's breast. She was born a few months earlier in Vistoso, a community two days' boat ride distant, which disappeared beneath a flooded river. That natural disaster led her father, a young hunter and trader of caiman skins, son of a mestizo businessman and an indigenous midwife, to seek a better life for his small family in this Amazonian city that, in those days, still retained some of the splendour of the rubber boom.

Mamita Lilí would later tell me that in her early childhood her grandfather Rafael Tuanama – my great-great-grandfather, a tall man with lighter eyes and skin than her – liked to sit in his deck chair, smoke his pipe and tell stories of his childhood, like when he went to the *shiringa* forests to trade the latex that Europe and the United States demanded by the ton to manufacture car tyres. The Amazonian indigenous peoples already knew of its properties: they had long used the sap of the *cauchuc* – the 'tree that weeps' in the Omagua language – to make balls and a kind of pipette for consuming narcotics and purgatives. With the arrival of the rubber business, however, whole villages were enslaved and set to work extracting the raw material that would modernise what became known as the First World.

While the rubber barons transformed Iquitos into a metropolis of European extravagance, with its steam-boats, mansions adorned with hand-painted Italian tiles, an opera house, and even a house made of iron purportedly designed by French engineer Gustave Eiffel, not far away the indigenous workers were opening up the jungle machete blow by machete blow, working from dawn to dusk, seeking out the rubber trees. Then, upon return to camp, they spent hours bent over the fire, inhaling acrid smoke, cooking the rubber until it formed a ball large enough to be sold. Countless native people were tricked when it came to their wages, paid in cheap liquor that kept them in a state of stupefaction, were beaten if they didn't comply, while others died of starvation, dysentery and other diseases, while their women and children were used as servants or to do unpaid work in the fields. Over all of this barbarity rose the splendour of Iquitos, known at that time as the 'Wall Street of Rubber'.

It was in this world of bonanzas and atrocities, where the indigenous people were seen as savages, almost as animals, deprived of intelligence and qualities, that my great-great-grandfather Rafael Tuanama worked. It was in the *shiringa* camps that he met the woman who would become his wife, Leonor Urquía, a Kukama-Kukamiria cook and midwife who accompanied him in everything he did. Mamita Lilí remembers that my great-great-grandfather, when drunk on aguardiente, would mock this brown-skinned woman with her angular cheekbones and narrow eyes, features inherited by their children and the children of their children.

'You should've turned out white like me,' Rafael said to his granddaughter Lilí, bragging about being the (illegitimate) son of a Spanish topographer, a white man. 'Your Indian grandma spoiled my lineage.'

To speak of rubber fever is not only to speak of thousands of human beings enslaved, tortured, displaced by entrepreneurs seeking to increase their wealth.

It was above all a system of oppression that reflected an aspect of late-nineteenth-century Western thought: the widespread idea that Amazonian societies were located at a lower stage of evolutionary development, a possible 'missing link' in the chain between monkey and human. Richard F. Burton, co-founder of the Anthropological Society of London, postulated that indigenous and black African peoples were 'subspecies'. Francis Galton, in his theory of eugenics – whose adherents included John Maynard Keynes and Winston Churchill – held that the indigenous peoples of the New World were 'mentally children'.

This racist thinking disguised as science was driven by large capital that financed explorations in lands where their interests were at stake, in the belief their mission was to bring 'progress' to these inhospitable jungles. In 1904, for example, the Peruvian government commissioned – through the mediation of Julio César Arana, the most powerful rubber baron of the period and owner of the Peruvian Amazon Company – the thirty-two-year-old explorer Eugène Robuchon, member of the Geographical Society of Paris, to carry out a geographical and anthropological study of the Putumayo region on the then disputed frontier with Colombia, at the epicentre of the rubber extraction industry.

For men like Robuchon – a passionate reader of Jules Verne who had spent his twenties criss-crossing South America – the Amazon natives were objects of study who aroused his curiosity and compassion, but also his fear and scorn: he considered them savages in need of civilising, a goal that extended to his personal life. His wife Hortensia was a young Araonas-Cavineños woman he met during an expedition through the Bolivian Amazon. He claimed to have saved from 'cannibals' his adoptive daughter Rita, who was of Bora ethnicity. In his first journeys through rubber territory – under the constant protection of armed men and of Othello, his Great Dane – Robuchon took photographs of the communities, wrote notes about their customs, recorded their languages on wax cylinders, took measurements of their bodies, and acquired their ritual and domestic objects in exchange for beads and knives. On the recommendation of his friend George Lomas, an English collector of 'ethnographic curiosities', he sent from Iquitos his showcase of objects, photographs and the manuscript with his notes (which posthumously was made into a book) to the British Museum most likely in 1905, awaiting a commission that never arrived. The following year, on a new journey of exploration in the Putumayo jungle, Robuchon disappeared without trace.

It was never clarified what had befallen him. Some said he got lost with his dog at some point along the Caquetá River, while his men went in search of provisions. Or that he died of hunger, and fell into the hands of 'cannibal Indians'. Other sources from the time suggest he was most likely murdered by the Arana Company: on his previous trip the French explorer had recorded in his notes and photographs the horrors committed against the indigenous people. Eliminating him was good for business. However, this did not prevent the rubber traders' crimes being learned of around the world.

In 1910 an investigation by the British Government verified that in the Putumayo jungle, the same region that Robuchon had disappeared in years earlier, the Peruvian Amazon Company had committed genocide in their attempt to pacify and enslave the Murui, Bora, Nonuya, Ocaina, Andoke, Resígaro and Muinane indigenous groups: they castrated and decapitated them, doused them with gasoline and set them on fire, crucified them upside down, flogged them, mutilated them, starved them to death, drowned them, and threw their remains to the dogs. The company's henchmen raped women and smashed open children's heads. All this was recounted by Roger Casement, the British consul general in charge of the investigation, and he estimated that some 30,000 indigenous people died at the hands of this company, known as 'the devil's paradise.'

More than a century later, the events of this period have left a deep wound in the memory of the indigenous peoples, the children and grandchildren of the survivors, a memory that in some way is also contained in the objects that explorers like Eugène Robuchon collected in these rivers and forests, though even today we have barely scratched the surface of their significance.

Of this collection today in the custody of the British Museum, comprising almost one hundred objects, only a couple of the works made with feathers have been put on display in temporary exhibitions. The rest of the material is poorly documented (Robuchon left only six half-size pages written in pencil recording the type of object and its origin) and is kept in Frank House, a four-storey building in London that contains hundreds of thousands of artefacts from across the planet that have not found a home in the museum's permanent exhibition.

To fill this void, in August 2019, Alicia Sánchez and Óscar Román, grandparents over eighty years of age, part of the generation of orphans left behind by the devastation of the Arana Company, crossed the Atlantic to visit the museum of one of the countries that financed the rubber industry in Putumayo. In the facilities of the British Museum's Santo Domingo Centre of Excellence for Latin American Research (SDCELAR), the elders of the Murui people (also known as Huitotos, a name given them by the white explorers), worked with the Colombian anthropologist Juan Álvaro Echévarri and reviewed the Murui-Bora collection which includes sixty-one objects sent by Robuchon: feather crowns, flutes, dance rattles, musical instruments made with turtle shells, jaguar-tooth necklaces, nose rings, raft ornaments, baskets, containers for hunting poison, and other pieces.

On a table covered with white paper, Echévarri relates, 'those objects did not seem to evoke either the history of violence nor the ritual and daily life of the peoples who had made them'. But thanks to the knowledge of Sánchez and Román, those items stopped being merely old things, things that in a crafts market could be nothing but exotic merchandise for a confused tourist, like those who visit the Amazon on holiday today. There are objects that need the context and the narration of their creators to acquire meaning.

Now we know, for example, that the red feathers of a crown are related to dance and ritual, to household things and to the act of caring and child-rearing. We know that the jaguar-tooth necklaces are related to the heat of animals, to the wild, aggression and war. We know that the trauma and pain of the rubber period belong to the 'basket of darkness', something that the descendants of the people affected by that barbarism prefer to leave closed, in order to open instead the 'basket of life', where the seeds of the future are enclosed.

The words of Óscar Román, one of the Murui wise men who recognised these items, sum up in their own way this intention:

'Kaieinamaki raana kiodikue jaa jiyodikue.'

'I saw the things of my ancestors and I was cured.'

'Do you recognise any of these objects?'

Beside an earthen road on the outskirts of Iquitos, at her stall selling chambira fibre bags, Liz Chicaje Churay, a Bora leader, peers at my laptop screen to examine the photos.

'That is the crown of the son of a chief, made with

the bright yellow feathers of a yellow-rumped cacique bird,' she says excitedly, seeing one of the items in the British Museum collection. 'And this larger one here, with black, white and reddish feathers, is from the breast of the toucan. To get coloured feathers like that, the birds are given special diets. But it's rarely done any more, that knowledge is being lost.'

Chicaje Churay, thirty-nine years old, is a descendant of the Newat (sparrowhawk) clan, part of the Bora nation, who are settled to the north of Loreto, and one of the few who survived the rubber genocide: prior to that period it is estimated they numbered some 18,000 people. Today, between Colombia and Peru barely 1,000 remain.

A mother to four boys and a girl named Cielo, Chicaje is a slender woman with bronze skin, a broad nose, straight hair tied in a ponytail and black eyes that shine when she speaks about the history of her people. In 2020 she was awarded the Goldman Prize, known as the 'Green Nobel' as it is granted to environmental leaders from the five continents, for persuading the Peruvian state to recognise the creation of the Yaguas National Park along the Colombian border, as a sacred place. A territory the size of 900 football pitches where wild animals can reproduce and communities subsist; intended to protect the river from illegal mining and halt the attacks of the timber traffickers, and to protect the lands where her ancestors are buried: Bora men and women who, in the early twentieth century, fled from the rubber barons who sought to enslave them. Her grandfather, Adolfo Churay, worked in the zone of La Chorrera, today a part of Colombia, close to the Putumayo. The same zone from where the explorer Eugène Robuchon took the items I'm showing her now on my screen.

The fact that the objects of her ancestors are exhibited today in the museums of the world's great capitals produces mixed feelings. On the one hand, she is proud because 'that way they can learn about my culture', but on the other she is sad at the reminder of the violence that led to these objects finding their way to the other side of the Atlantic. A painful memory, she tells me, like that of the massacre of thousands of peasants in the Andes during the war against the terrorism of the Sendero Luminoso in Peru in the 1980s.

'When I see photographs from that period, how they killed without pity, how they treated us as beasts, as Indians... The memory causes rage. The worst thing is to continue receiving this treatment from mestizos and from white people when we demand our rights.'

Chicaje remembers the time she visited the regional president of Loreto in 2015 to demand he approve the creation of the national park that would protect her ancestral forests. 'Why do the Indians want more forests?' she remembers the official asking with a sneer of irritation. 'Don't they know I can send for a thousand chainsaws and cut these trees down?'

Since then, she has met with similar treatment countless times. Above all from authorities who see only timber in the forest: resources to exploit and sell to the highest bidder, without caring that hundreds of families live in, from and for these forests, and have done for generations.

That is why what most concerns her today is the gradual loss of this memory. In her community of Pucaurquillo (a day by boat from Iquitos, and home to 250 Bora and Huitoto families), she sees that the young people, even her own children, are losing interest in their culture. The young ones leave for the city to look for work. Some go to Lima, others to Colombia, 'and there, everything is in Spanish,' says Chicaje, 'they are embarrassed to speak their own language'.

'This knowledge is being lost, and it worries me greatly. I want to ask my grandma Marcela, who is eighty-seven, the meaning of these things, of the paintings, the weavings. We know the myths, but very little now. I have to get as much as possible out of my grandmother before she dies.'

She knows that when a language dies a way of life and of being in the world dies with it: a way of knowing it and speaking of it.

There is a historical memory that the Amazonian people seek to preserve. A memory that is outside of museums, that cannot be contained in walls or artefacts, that struggles to endure, and which is their most urgent focus of attention. My friend Liz Chicaje tries to do this work, recording the testimony, the wisdom of her grandmother. She feels that this account completes, in some way, what she is.

How I would have loved to do the same with Mamita Lilí. How I wish I'd had the time to get to know her. The only memories of my grandmother in this jungle, the vague memory of her past working with the rubber, her father the caiman hunter, her migration to Lima, her years trying to survive in a society that treats the indigenous as something inferior, are preserved in the hours of conversations I recorded. Audio recordings that only recently, in order to write these lines, I dared to listen to for the first time.

I remember that at the end of a journey we made to Pucallpa, another Amazonian city where she spent part of her childhood, days before I moved to Barcelona to write my first book, we promised we would come to Iquitos to go and look for Vistoso. We wanted to find out what remained of the community she was born in. She also passed on to me old photographs, her birth certificate, fragments of memory. It was the last time I saw her. Not long after, Mamita Lilí died of cancer. She was seventy-eight years old.

Now, the evening sky over the Belén neighbourhood is clear of clouds. The setting sun heightens every colour.

A Facebook notification pops up with a photograph I took of Mamita Lilí on that last trip, in a port not unlike this one: she is standing, smiling, clinging to my mother's arm, with her red coat, her walking stick, surrounded by clusters of green bananas. The Ucayali flows imperturbably behind her.

Three years later, on the anniversary of her death, my mother and I would escape from Lima to take a photograph of ourselves on the same spot. I look for it on my phone. Save for a few details, it's the same image. There are the boats, the green bananas. The brown river. But without her. Sooner or later we will all be that person missing in photographs.

AUTHOR BIOGRAPHIES

Yásnaya Elena A. Gil (Ayutla Mixe, Mexico, 1981) is part of COLMIX, a group of young Mixe people dedicated to researching, communicating and promoting Mixe language, history and culture. She studied Hispanic Language and Literatures and received a Masters in Linguistics at the National Autonomous University of Mexico. She has collaborated in various projects around linguistic diversity, the development of grammar content for educational materials in indigenous languages, and projects documenting languages at risk of disappearance. She has helped develop written materials in Mixe as well as building readerships in Mixe and other indigenous languages. As an activist she has defended the linguistic rights of speakers of indigenous languages, and promoted the use of them online and in literary translation.

Gabriela Cabezón Cámara (Buenos Aires, Argentina, 1968) has practised many trades – from selling car insurance on the street, to designing newspaper layouts – the most relevant for the current purposes being cultural journalism and teaching – for want of a better word – creative writing. She currently runs the Laboratorio de Experimentación de Artes de la Escritura at the National University of the Arts in Buenos Aires. She has always been involved in activism and militancy, and today her most pressing cause is the resistance to the Capitalocene: the fight to protect all living things. Her novels and novellas include *La Virgen Cabeza, Le viste la cara a Dios, Romance de la Negra Rubia* and *Las aventuras de la China*

Iron. The English translation of the latter, *The Adventures of China Iron*, was shortlisted for the 2020 International Booker Prize. The French translation was shortlisted for the 2021 Foreign Language Prix Mèdicis. Her work has been translated into English, French, Norwegian, Portuguese and Italian, and Turkish, Greek, Lithuanian, Slovenian and Croatian editions of her books are forthcoming.

Juan Cárdenas (Popayán, Colombia, 1978) is the author of the novels *Zumbido* (451 Editores, 2010 / Periférica, 2017), *Los estratos* (Periférica, 2013), *Ornamento* (Periférica, 2015), *Tú y yo, una novelita rusa* (Cajón de Sastre, 2016), *El diablo de las provincias* (Periférica, 2017) and *Elástico de sombra* (Sexto Piso, 2019). He also wrote the book of short stories *Volver a comer del árbol de la ciencia* (Tusquets, 2018). He is currently a teacher and researcher on the Creative Writing Masters Programme at The Caro and Cuervo Institute, Bogotá.

Carlos Fonseca (San José, Costa Rica, 1987) is the author of the novels *Coronel Lágrimas* (Anagrama, 2015) and *Museo animal* (Anagrama, 2017), as well as the essay *La lucidez del miope* (Germinal, 2017), which won the National Prize for Literature in Costa Rica. In 2016 he was selected by the Guadalajara Book Fair as one of the twenty most promising Latin American authors born in the eighties. In 2017, he was selected on the Bogotá–39 list, comprising thirty-nine of the most promising writers under forty in Latin America. In 2020 he was selected as part of the Granta list naming the twenty-five best writers in the Spanish language. His latest novel, *Austral*, will be published by Anagrama in 2022. He is a professor and fellow at Trinity College, Cambridge University.

Lina Meruane (Santiago de Chile, Chile, 1970) is the author of two short story collections, *Las infantas* and *Avidez*, and five novels: *Póstuma, Cercada, Fruta podrida, Sangre en el ojo* and *Sistema nervioso*. Her non-fiction books include the essays *Viajes virales* and *Zona ciega*, as well as the personal essay *Volverse Palestina*, the lyrical essay *Palestina*, and the diatribe *Against Children*. She has received the Cálamo Prize (Spain, 2016), the Sor Juana Inés de la Cruz Prize (Mexico 2012), the Anna Seghers Prize (Berlin 2011) and writing grants from the Guggenheim Foundation (USA 2004), the NEA (USA 2010), the DAAD (Berlin 2017), and Casa Cien Años de Soledad (Mexico 2021), among others. She currently teaches at NYU Madrid.

Dolores Reyes (Buenos Aires, Argentina, 1978) studied to be a primary school teacher, as well as Greek and Classical Cultures at the University of Buenos Aires. She worked on her first novel *Cometierra* with Selva Almada and Julian López. The novel was published in 2019 in Argentina and Spain by Editorial Sigilo and in Colombia by Rey Naranjo and was a finalist for the Medifé-Filba Foundation Novel Prize, the Silverio Cañada Memorial Prize, the Mario Vargas Llosa Prize and the Sara Gallardo National Novel Prize. *Cometierra* was translated and published into English, Italian, French, Swedish and Polish, and it is forthcoming in Dutch, Greek, Portuguese, Norwegian and Danish. Dolores Reyes currently teaches writing workshops and is writing a storybook and a sequel to *Cometierra*.

Djamila Ribeiro (Santos, Brazil, 1980) holds a degree in Philosophy and a Masters in Political Philosophy from the Federal University of São Paulo. Author of the books *Lugar de fala* (Place of Speech), *Quem tem medo* *do feminismo negro?* (Who's Afraid of Black Feminism?), *Pequeno manual antirracista* (Short Anti-Racist Guide) and *Cartas para minha avó* (Letters to my Grandmother), with translations into four languages. She is also a visiting professor at the department of journalism at the Pontifical Catholic University of São Paulo (PUC-SP) and currently a fellow at the Johannes Gutenberg University Mainz, Germany. Columnist for *Folha de São Paulo* newspaper and *ELLE* Brazil magazine, she was deputy secretary for Human Rights in São Paulo in 2016. She was awarded the 2019 Prince Claus Prize, granted by the Netherlands and was considered by the BBC as one of the 100 most influential women in the world. In 2020, she won the Jabuti Prize in the Human Science category, with her book *Pequeno manual antirracista*. In 2021, she was the first Brazilian to be honoured by the BET Awards, given by the black community of the USA.

Cristina Rivera Garza (Matamoros, Mexico, 1964) is an author, translator and critic. Her recent publications include *El invencible verano de Liliana* (PRH, 2021) and *Autobiografía del algodón* (PRH, 2020). Her book *Grieving: Dispatches from a Wounded Country*, translated by Sarah Booker, was shortlisted for the NBCC award in 2021. Her book of *New and Selected Stories* was published by Dorothy Project in 2022. She became a MacArthur Fellow in 2020, and is the recipient of the International Donoso Literary Award 2021. Rivera Garza is Distinguished Professor and founder of the PhD Program in Creative Writing in Spanish at the University of Houston, Department of Hispanic Studies.

Velia Vidal (Bahía Solano, Colombia, 1982) is a writer who loves the sea and shared readings. In 2021 she was a fellow at Villa Josepha Ahrenshoop, in Germany. For her book *Aguas de estuario* (Laguna Libros, 2020) she won the Afro-Colombian Authors Publication Grant awarded by Colombia's Ministry of Culture. She is the co-author of *Oír somos río* (2019) and its bilingual German-Spanish edition (Grindwal Kollektiv, 2021). She published the children's story *Bajo el yarumo*, as part of the *Maletín de relatos pacíficos* collection (Instituto Caro y Cuervo, Fondo Acción, 2017). She is the founder and director of the Motete Educational and Cultural Corporation and the Chocó Reading and Writing Festival (FLECHO). Vidal graduated in Afro-Latin American Studies and has a Masters in Reading Education and Children's Literature. She is also a journalist and specialist in social management and communication.

Joseph Zárate (Lima, Peru, 1986) is a journalist and editor. He is the recipient of a 2018 Gabriel García Márquez Award, the 2016 Ortega y Gasset Award for Best Story or Journalistic Investigation and the PAGE 2015 National Award for Environmental Journalism. He has a Masters in Literary Creation from Pompeu Fabra University in Barcelona and received the 2018 Ochberg Fellowship from the Dart Center for Journalism and Trauma at the Columbia University School of Journalism in New York. He is currently a professor of Literary Journalism at the Peruvian University of Applied Sciences. He is the author of *Guerras del interior* (2018), which has been translated into English, Italian and Polish. In 2020 he won the National Journalism Prize and was nominated for the 2020/21 True Story Award for his long-form journalism about funeral workers during the Covid-19 pandemic in Peru.

TRANSLATOR BIOGRAPHIES

Daniel Hahn is a writer, editor and translator with over eighty books to his name. His translations (from Portuguese, Spanish and French) include fiction from Europe, Africa and the Americas and non-fiction by writers ranging from Portuguese Nobel laureate José Saramago to Brazilian footballer Pelé. He is a former chair of the Society of Authors and is presently on the board of a number of organisations that deal with literature, literacy, translation and free expression. In 2020 Daniel was made an OBE for services to literature.

Ellen Jones is a writer, editor, and literary translator from Spanish. Her recent and forthcoming translations include *Cubanthropy* by Iván de la Nuez (Seven Stories Press, 2023), *The Forgery* by Ave Barrera (Charco Press, 2022, co-translated with Robin Myers), and *Nancy* by Bruno Lloret (Two Lines Press, 2021). Her monograph, *Literature in Motion: Translating Multilingualism Across the Americas* is published by Columbia University Press (2022).

Christina MacSweeney received the 2016 Valle Inclán prize for her translation of Valeria Luiselli's *The Story of My Teeth*, and her translation of Daniel Saldaña París' *Among Strange Victims* was a finalist for the 2017 Best Translated Book Award. Other authors she has translated include: Jazmina Barrera (*On Lighthouses*; *Linea Nigra*), Elvira Navarro (*A Working Woman*), Verónica Gerber Bicecci (*Empty Set*; *Palabras migrantes / Migrant Words*), and

Julián Herbert (*Tomb Song; The House of the Pain of Others*). Christina has also contributed to several anthologies of translated literature and has published shorter translations of prose and poetry, interviews and articles on a wide variety of platforms. Her translation of Valeria Luiselli's *Faces in the Crowd* was adapted for the stage at the Gate Theatre, London, in 2020.

Annie McDermott is a literary translator working from Spanish and Portuguese into English. Her recent translations include *The Luminous Novel* and *Empty Words* by Mario Levrero, *Brickmakers* and *Dead Girls* by Selva Almada, *Wars of the Interior* by Joseph Zárate and *The Wind Whistling in the Cranes* by Lídia Jorge (co-translation with Margaret Jull Costa). Her work has been shortlisted for the Premio Valle Inclán and the Harvill Secker Young Translators' Prize. She has previously lived in Mexico City and São Paulo, Brazil, and is now based in Hastings, in the UK.

Megan McDowell has translated many of the most important Latin American writers working today, including Samanta Schweblin, Alejandro Zambra, Mariana Enriquez, and Lina Meruane. Her translations have won the English PEN award, the Premio Valle Inclán, and the Shirley Jackson Prize, and have been short- or long-listed four times for the International Booker Prize, and shortlisted once for the Kirkus Prize. In 2020 she won an Award in Literature from the American Academy of Arts and Letters. Her short story translations have been featured in The New Yorker, Harper's, The Paris Review, Tin House, McSweeney's, and Granta, among others. She is from Richmond, KY and lives in Santiago, Chile.

Robin Myers is a poet and Spanish-to-English translator. Her translations include *Copy* by Dolores Dorantes (Wave Books), *The Dream of Every Cell* by Maricela Guerrero (Cardboard House Press), *The Book of Explanations* by Tedi López Mills (Deep Vellum Publishing), *Cars on Fire* by Mónica Ramón Ríos (Open Letter Books), *The Restless Dead* by Cristina Rivera Garza (Vanderbilt University Press), and other works of poetry and prose. She was a winner of the 2019 Poems in Translation Contest (Words Without Borders/Academy of American Poets). Other translations have appeared in the *Kenyon Review*, *The Common*, *Harvard Review*, *Two Lines*, *Waxwing*, *Asymptote*, *Los Angeles Review of Books*, *The Baffler*, and elsewhere. She lives in Mexico City.

Carolina Orloff is a translator and researcher in Latin American literature, who has published extensively on Julio Cortázar as well as on Latin American literature, and cinema. In 2016, after obtaining her PhD in Latin American Literature from the University of Edinburgh and working in the academic sector, Carolina co-founded Charco Press where she acts as editorial director. She is also the co-translator of *Fate* by Jorge Consiglio and of Ariana Harwicz's *Die, My Love*, which was longlisted for the Man Booker International 2018. For her work as editor in Charco Press, Carolina was named 'Emerging Publisher of the Year' by the Saltire Society in 2018.

Fionn Petch is a Scottish-born translator working from Spanish, French, and Italian into English. He lived in Mexico City for 12 years, where he completed a PhD in Philosophy at the National Autonomous University of Mexico, and now lives in Berlin. His translations of Latin American literature for Charco Press have been widely acclaimed. *Fireflies* by Luis Sagasti was shortlisted for the Translators' Association First Translation Award 2018. *The Distance Between Us* by Renato Cisneros received an English PEN Award in 2018. *A Musical Offering*, also by Luis Sagasti, was shortlisted for the Republic of Consciousness Prize 2021 and won the UK Society of Authors Premio Valle Inclán 2021 for best translation from Spanish.

Frances Riddle has translated numerous Spanish-language authors including Isabel Allende, Claudia Piñeiro, Leila Guerriero, and Sara Gallardo. Her translation of *Elena Knows* by Claudia Piñeiro was shortlisted for the International Booker Prize in 2022 and her translation of *Theatre of War* by Andrea Jeftanovic was granted an English PEN Award in 2020. Her work has appeared in journals such as *Granta*, *Electric Literature*, and *The White Review*, among others. She holds a BA in Spanish Language and Literature from Louisiana State University and an MA in Translation Studies from the University of Buenos Aires. Originally from Houston, Texas she lives in Buenos Aires, Argentina.

Frank Wynne is a literary translator. Born in Ireland, he moved to France in 1984 where he discovered a passion for language. He worked as a bookseller in Paris and again when he moved to London in 1987, he translated and published comics and graphic novels and from 1996-2001 he worked in online media. He began translating literature in the late 1990s, and in 2001 decided to devote himself to this full time. He has translated works by, among others, Michel Houellebecq, Frédéric Beigbeder, Ahmadou Kourouma, Boualem Sansal, Claude Lanzmann, Tomás Eloy Martínez and Almudena Grandes. His work has earned him several awards, including the

Scott Moncrieff Prize and the Premio Valle Inclán. Most recently, his translation of *Vernon Subutex* was shortlisted for the Man Booker International 2018.

CURATOR BIOGRAPHIES

Laura Osorio Sunnucks is Head of the Santo Domingo Centre of Excellence for Latin American Research at the British Museum. Previously she was Mellon Postdoctoral Curatorial Fellow for Latin America at the Museum of Anthropology (MOA), University of British Columbia, where she created a field collection and curated the exhibition 'Arts of Resistance; Politics and the Past in Latin America.' She has also worked on the Indigenous and Minority Fellowship Programme at UNESCO Paris and in Anglophone education at the Louvre Museum. She holds a PhD in Mesoamerican heritage from Leiden University. This ongoing work with Maya specialists in Yucatan champions the inclusion of local practices and theories in the interpretation of archaeological sites and historical materials in the region.

María Mercedes Martínez Milantchi is Project Coordinator for the Santo Domingo Centre of Excellence for Latin American Research at the British Museum. She holds a Bachelor of Arts from Yale University and an Erasmus Mundus masters in ARCHaeological MATerial Sciences (University of Evora, Sapienza University & Aristotle University) with a focus on pre-Columbian Caribbean archaeology. Previously, she has experience working and researching at the Smithsonian's Office of International Relations & Museum Conservation Institute, the Yale Art Gallery, and the Peabody Museum of Natural History. Her current research focuses on the archaeology and materialities of European/Indigenous encounter.

Magdalena Araus Sieber is Digital Curator for the Santo Domingo Centre of Excellence for Latin American Research at the British Museum. She holds a Bachelor of Arts in History from Universidad Católica de Chile, an Education degree from Universidad Gabriel Mistral and a Digital Humanities Masters, with focus on museums and technologies, from University College London. Her professional background combines editorial management in digital journalism and exhibitions renovation at the National Museums Department in Chile. She is interested in technologies and digital platforms that enhance learning experiences and engage non-specialised audiences in museums.

IMAGE CREDITS

ACKNOWLEDGEMENTS

Izara García, International Coordinator, Hay Festival

Sophie Hughes, literary coordinator of the Anagrama edition

Carolina Orloff, publisher at Charco Press and editor and coordinator of the English edition

Zoe Romero, Inaki Lasa, Christopher Bone, Hay Festival international team

Felipe Restrepo Pombo, editor of the Spanish edition

Silvia Sesé and Lluïsa Matarrodona, editors at Anagrama

Director & Editor: Carolina Orloff
Director: Samuel McDowell

www.charcopress.com

Untold Microcosms was published on
80gsm Munken Premium Cream paper.

The text was designed using Bembo 11.5 and ITC Galliard.

Printed in July 2022 by TJ Books
Padstow, Cornwall, PL28 8RW using responsibly
sourced paper and environmentally-friendly adhesive.